CULTURES OF THE WORLD

FRANCE

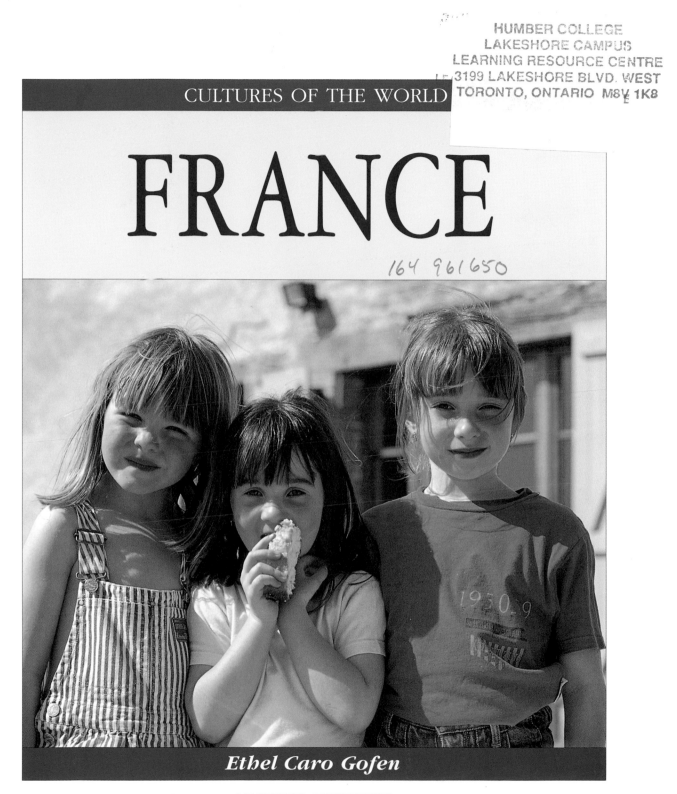

Ethel Caro Gofen

MARSHALL CAVENDISH
New York • London • Sydney

Reference edition published 1993 by
Marshall Cavendish Corporation
2415 Jerusalem Avenue
P.O. Box 587
North Bellmore
New York 11710

Originated and designed by
Times Books International, an imprint of
Times Editions Pte Ltd

Printed in Singapore

Library of Congress Cataloging-in-Publication Data:
Gofen, Ethel, 1937–
    France / Ethel Caro Gofen.
        p. cm.—(Cultures Of The World)
    Includes bibliographical references and index.
    Summary: An overview of the geography,
history, government, culture, and people of
France.
    ISBN 1-85435-449-3
    1. France—Juvenile literature. [1. France.]
I. Title. II. Series.
DC33.G54 1992
944—dc20   91–40376
                    CIP
                        AC

Cultures of the World

Editorial Director	Shirley Hew
Managing Editor	Shova Loh
Editors	Roseline Lum
	Goh Sui Noi
	June Khoo Ai Lin
	Siow Peng Han
	Leonard Lau
	Tan Kok Eng
	MaryLee Knowlton
Picture Editor	Yee May Kaung
Production	Edmund Lam
Design	Tuck Loong
	Ang Siew Lian
	Lee Woon Hong
	Lo Yen Yen
	Ong Su Ping
Illustrators	Suzana Fong
	Kelvin Sim
Cover Picture	Nicola Sutton (Life File)

INTRODUCTION

 FRANCE IS A LAND of incredible beauty. From Paris to the Alpine glaciers, from the beaches of Normandy to the flower-strewn hills of Provence, wherever one travels in France, its vistas are varied and dramatically picturesque.

The energetic, well-educated French people believe their country is the noblest and best in the world. Their achievements in architecture, literature, painting, fashion, cooking and wine making have dazzled the rest of the world. Perhaps their greatest creative achievement is the art of living joyfully.

The French have experienced many different forms of government in their tumultuous history. They were ruled by kings, emperors, a consul and presidents of five successive republics. They learned to defend the rights of the individual against all forms of tyranny and gave the world the precious concepts of Liberty, Equality and Fraternity.

This book, part of the series *Cultures of the World*, provides insights into the lifestyle of the French people and their dynamic intellectual and cultural achievements.

PARIS

CONTENTS

Saint-Tropez on the Côte d'Azur is a favorite vacation spot for thousands of French people and tourists.

CONTENTS

Versailles is one of the most beautiful palaces in the world.

GEOGRAPHY

FRANCE IS BLESSED WITH FERTILE SOIL and a pleasant climate. In France, you'll find a great diversity of land forms: snow-capped mountain ranges, broad plains, dense forests, windblown seacoasts, extinct volcanic cones, mysterious underground ancient caves and sunny Mediterranean beaches.

The country resembles a hexagon in shape and covers 210,026 square miles. It is roughly 600 miles long and close to 600 miles across at its widest point. The island of Corsica, southeast of mainland France in the Mediterranean Sea, accounts for 3,367 square miles of the total land area.

France's bordering neighbors are Belgium, Luxembourg and Germany on the northeast, Switzerland and Italy to the east and southeast, Andorra on the south, and Spain on the southwest. Half of the country's borders are coastlines, with the Atlantic Ocean and the Bay of Biscay to the west, the English Channel to the northwest and the Mediterranean Sea to the southeast.

Most of France's boundaries are natural—the Pyrenees Mountains leading into Spain, the Alps and Jura Mountains bordering Switzerland, and more Alpine peaks between France and Italy. The Rhine River flows between France and Germany.

Opposite: **Mont-Saint-Michel is a very small island off the coast of Normandy. It is topped by an abbey of the same name.**

Above: **The coast of Brittany contains many tranquil little coves which can get quite crowded during summer vacations.**

The Alps act as a natural border between France and Switzerland. The highest mountain in Western Europe is Mont Blanc on the French side of the Alps.

Where no natural barriers exist, France has been vulnerable to invasion by foreign armies, most recently by the Nazis during World War II. In these areas, the boundaries have shifted many times as a result of wars.

The highest point in the country—in fact, in the whole of Western Europe—is the peak of Mont Blanc (15,771 feet) in the French Alps. The lowest area in France is the Rhône River delta, below sea level.

NINE MAIN LAND REGIONS

The widely varied landscapes of mainland France can be divided into nine different regions, each with its particular beauty:

THE BRITTANY-NORMANDY HILLS lie in northwestern France across the eroded remains of ancient rock. Low hills and rolling plains are covered with relatively infertile soil. The rugged coastline is dotted with many bays and is home to both tiny fishing villages and the major seaports of Le Havre and Cherbourg. Important products of this region include apples, used to make cider and an alcoholic drink called Calvados, dairy foods such as Camembert cheese and Normandy butter, and fish.

Brittany, with the highest percentage of Catholic church-goers of any French region, has also spawned a small group of extremist Bretons who want to separate from the rest of the country. The ancient Celtic language is still spoken here, and mysterious standing stones recall the ancestors.

THE NORTHERN FRANCE PLAINS include the capital city of Paris, the cultural and intellectual center of all France. In one sense, it is also a geographical center since all distances in France are measured from the square in front of Notre-Dame Cathedral.

A gap between two boulders is put to good use at Plougrescant in Brittany.

Surrounding Paris is the Paris Basin, also known as the Ile-de-France. Its rich farmland and major industries support a dense population.

Formerly important industries in this part of France include textiles in the northern city of Lille and coal-mining near the Belgian border. The metropolitan area of Lille-Roubaix-Tourcoing is one of France's largest provincial centers of population, with about 1 million people.

THE NORTHEASTERN PLATEAUS include the provinces of Alsace and Lorraine. These plateaus are crossed by the Ardennes and Vosges mountain ranges. Farming and vineyards dominate the lower slopes and valleys. Rich iron ore deposits and heavy forests brought lumbering and iron and steel production to the area, though mining is now in decline.

Nice is a prosperous town and its port is always teeming with yachts and other pleasure boats.

THE RHÔNE-SAÔNE VALLEY is dominated by the city of Lyon, which, like Lille and Marseilles, is home to roughly 1 million people. Lyon has been famous for many centuries for its tradition of great cooking and its silk and synthetic fabric production.

THE FRENCH ALPS AND JURA MOUNTAINS boast many ski resorts. Mountain streams have been harnessed to bring hydroelectric power to farms and industries. A range of Alpine peaks known as the Massif du Mont Blanc soars above 13,000 feet, crowned by the highest peak, Mont Blanc.

THE RIVIERA is an international playground of great beauty. A visitor to these parts can sample all altitudes, from mountains to charming hill towns down to a coastal plain and sandy beaches. Marseilles, France's chief seaport, and the tiny independent country of Monaco are in this area, as are the renowned resort cities of Nice and Cannes.

Awesome Roman ruins, medieval buildings, ancient olive groves and even bullfight arenas mark the inland region of Provence. Many famous French artists have tried to capture its luminous daylight.

THE MASSIF CENTRAL is the largest of France's geographic sections, covering one-sixth of the country. High granite plateaus are cut in many places by deep gorges. Extinct volcanic cones known as *puys*, some topped with chapels or religious statues, are a striking feature of the area. At Vichy, natural hot mineral springs have led to the development of health spas. Its bottled mineral water is exported to distant countries.

Where the soil is poor, most of the Massif Central tends to be thinly populated. In recent years, many people from this part of France have moved to Paris to look for jobs.

THE PYRENEES MOUNTAINS separate France and Spain in a sparsely populated region of the southwest. Many of the mountain peaks top 10,000 feet. Farmers raise cattle and sheep in this area. The Pyrenees town of Lourdes attracts millions of Roman Catholic pilgrims, drawn by its reputation for miraculous cures.

THE AQUITANIAN LOWLANDS region is known for its fruit orchards, the Bordeaux wine industry, oil and natural gas fields, steel mills and chemical factories. The seaport of Bordeaux and the aerospace industry center of Toulouse are here. Famous brandies originate in towns of the same name: Cognac and Armagnac. Extensive forests, rolling plains, huge sand dunes and beaches are characteristic features of this area.

Almond trees in full bloom in the Roussillon region as the Pyrenees loom with majestic grandeur in the background.

A COUNTRY NOURISHED BY WATER

France's important rivers include the Loire, the Seine, the Rhône, the Garonne, the Rhine, the Somme, the Saône and the Marne. The <u>Loire</u> is the longest river entirely within France: 650 miles long. Glorious *châteaux,* or castles, adorn its banks.

Throughout French history, rivers have brought fertility to the land and have nourished flourishing centers of population. These rivers, with their lesser tributaries and a vast system of linking canals, have enabled the French to cross their country by boat and barge for hundreds of years.

The Seine connects Paris with the Atlantic Ocean. Rouen, the capital of Normandy and a busy industrial center, is also on the Seine. Bordeaux, the great wine center and seaport, lies on the Garonne. Its location makes it an ideal home for merchants and shipbuilders.

Lyon lies at the point where the Rhône and Saône rivers meet, and its heart is a peninsula between the two rivers. Since the Rhône-Saône Valley receives relatively little rainfall, the Rhône provides both hydroelectric power and irrigation to farms and vineyards in that region. The Rhine brings hydroelectric power to the Alsace-Lorraine region.

A complex system of canals eases the flow of goods between the smaller cities and towns. Some examples are the Nantes-Brest Canal in Brittany, the Canal du Nivernais in Burgundy, and the Canal du Midi, running from Toulouse to the Languedoc coast.

FRENCH INFLUENCE CIRCLES THE GLOBE

The French Republic also governs a number of overseas departments and territories. Mostly former French colonies, they reflect the far-flung influence of French civilization during the country's greatest expansion.

Departments abroad include Guadeloupe and Martinique in the Caribbean, French Guiana in South America, and Réunion in the Indian Ocean. The people of these lands are considered French citizens, and they elect representatives to the French Parliament in Paris.

Mayotte and Saint Pierre and Miquelon are called territorial collectivities. French territories include New Caledonia, French Polynesia, and Wallis and Futuna Islands in the South Pacific, and the French Southern and Antarctic holdings in the Indian Ocean and Antarctica.

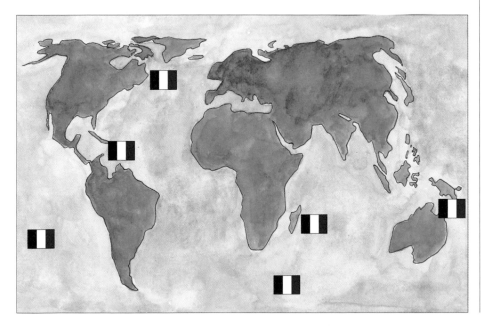

Although France has lost most of its colonies, various islands in different parts of the world are still under French jurisdiction.

CORSICA SEEKS A SEPARATE IDENTITY

Corsica lies in the Mediterranean Sea about 100 miles from mainland France. Some visitors find it more Italian than French, and, in fact, it is merely 50 miles west of the Italian mainland. Over the centuries, Corsica has belonged to invaders from Greece, Rome, Pisa and finally Genoa. In 1769, Genoa sold its rights to Corsica to the French, and the island became a department of the French Republic.

Corsica's coast is marked by steep, rocky cliffs leading up to rugged mountains. Poor soil and heavy forests limit the amount of land given to agricultural use. The people fish, raise sheep and some farm crops and work in industries based on hydroelectric development. Tobacco-growing supports about one-quarter of the economy.

Tourists enjoy sandy beaches with palm trees and dramatic scenic drives. Many interesting villages inland have remained almost unchanged for hundreds of years. Some small settlements along the coastal bays can be reached only by boat.

Napoleon Bonaparte, Corsica's most famous citizen who later became emperor of the French people, was born in the capital city of Ajaccio.

In Corsica, traditional loyalties to family and clan have led to lengthy, sometimes deadly, revenge-seeking vendettas. In fact, the word "vendetta," meaning a hereditary blood feud, came into the English language from Corsica.

Most recently, Corsican zeal has also inspired a long guerrilla battle for greater autonomy and cultural recognition. The Corsican language, a form of Italian, is widely spoken at home although the French banned it from the schools. Corsican nationalists have not hesitated to use terrorist tactics to further their separatist aims.

In 1991, French lawmakers adopted an article that named Corsicans the "Corsican people, a component of the French people." However it was invalidated by the Constitutional Council, which makes sure that all the laws passed are within the constitution.

CLIMATE

The climate of each region depends on its distance from the sea and its relation to the mountains. The western part of the country receives winds off the Atlantic Ocean that bring rain and cool winters (44 F average) with moderate summers (around 60 F). The Gulf Stream in the Atlantic Ocean is responsible for tempering the climate and making it warmer and more moderate than at comparable longitudes in North America. A light misty rain is common through most of the year.

The Provence region has a warm climate that supports lush tropical greenery.

Inland, there is a more pronounced seasonal difference, with hotter summers and colder winters, and with clearly defined wet and dry periods. In the Paris Basin, the average yearly temperature is 53 F.

Eastern France experiences more severe winters and stormy summers than the western and middle regions. The Vosges Mountains affect the region of Alsace, causing its sharp cold winters and warm to hot summers.

The mountain areas have the most severe extremes of weather. Often peaks remain snow-covered, with glaciers appearing in the Alps. The mountains also receive more rain, reaching more than 55 inches annually. By contrast, the rainfall along the Mediterranean coast is only 25 inches.

The Riviera with its dry, warm climate is well-protected by the Alps. Summers are dry and hot, with temperatures soaring into the 90s. Still, cold north winds known as *mistrals* sometimes blow through southeastern France at a brutal 65 miles per hour—enough force to threaten the crops.

There is a profusion of flowers in France. Some are used in the perfume industry; others, like the sunflower, are used to produce oil.

NATIVE PLANTS

The native trees and plants of France vary with the climate from one part of the country to another. In the northern and central regions, forests of oak and beech trees are common. In the low-lying marshes, willows, poplar, pine and birch trees may be found.

On the western border, carefully planted pine forests thrive where swamps have been drained. The Brittany landscape, so commonly a bleak expanse of moors with scrubby brush and stunted trees, contrasts greatly with the Provençal landscape of ancient olive trees and verdant grapevines and fruit trees. In other parts of France, cypress, Spanish chestnut and ash trees form thick groves and forests. Evergreens such as cushion pine, dwarf pine and juniper flourish in parts of the Alps.

More than one-third of the country is planted for agriculture. Wheat, barley and corn are among the chief crops. Lavender, thyme and other herbs, hidden truffles and mushrooms in rich variety scent the fields and flavor the tables of France.

NATIVE ANIMALS

The shellfish of the north coast and trout and salmon of the Pyrenees waters please diners throughout the land. Game birds of all kinds attract both hunters and adventurous eaters. More unusual than tasty are the flamingos, herons and storks that ripple the lake waters of nature preserves in the province of Lorraine.

Wild animals include the brown bear, wild boar, polecat, wildcat and deer. The wild horses in the marshy Camargue region of Provence are a particularly dramatic sight. Among the smaller mammals commonly seen in the French countryside are badgers, bats, beavers, foxes, hares, hedgehogs, moles, rabbits, squirrels and weasels. Farmers depend on more common animals for a living: cattle, chickens, hogs and sheep.

The horses bred in the Camargue region are smaller than usual. Their rapid reflexes, endurance and agility make them ideal for working with bulls.

HISTORY

TWO THEMES dominate French history. One is the drive to forge a unified nation out of diverse peoples; the second is the quest for glory. France wanted, and still wants, to embody the most cultured and enlightened civilization in the world.

EARLY SETTLERS

"Cavemen" inhabited the region as far back as 750,000 years ago. The first tribes to invade France were the Celts. Megalithic monuments and Celtic words in the French language recall these people, who were later known as Gauls.

In 52 B.C., Julius Caesar defeated the Gallic chief Vercingetorix. Rome ruled the area for the next 500 years. The Romans built extensive roads, towns and cities. They also left a legal system, taxes and the art of wine-making. Latin became the foundation of the modern French language.

In the 5th century A.D., Visigoths, Burgundians and Franks pushed their way into France. The Visigoths settled in the southwest. The Burgundians stayed in the eastern region now known as Burgundy. The Franks settled in the northeast around present-day Paris.

It was the Franks, under Clovis, who finally drove the Romans away. They gave the country its name of France. Clovis founded the French monarchy, chose Paris as its capital, and converted to Catholicism.

Charlemagne, who ruled from 768 to 814, dreamed of re-establishing the Roman Empire with Christian ideals. He was crowned emperor in 800 and controlled the largest expanse of territory since the Roman period.

After Charlemagne died, his empire was divided among his three grandsons. The three parts had the rough outlines of what later became modern Germany, modern France, and a combination of modern Holland, Belgium, Alsace-Lorraine and northern Italy.

Opposite: **The concept of the arc of triumph is of Roman origin. The most well-known is the Arc de Triomphe de l'Etoile, whose construction was ordered by Napoleon after he won the battle of Austerlitz. It contains several remarkable sculptures.**

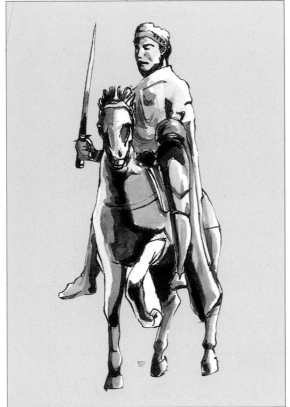

Many nobles left France to fight in the Crusades and recapture the Holy Land from the Moslems. The French monarchy took this opportunity to seize the land and the power of the crusading nobles.

THE MIDDLE AGES

In 987 powerful nobles ended the Carolingian line of kings and named Hugh Capet king. The rule of the Capetians lasted from the 10th to the 14th century, a period known as the Middle Ages. Hugh Capet established the principle of primogeniture, by which the oldest son inherits everything. This led to a more orderly succession of power.

In the 10th century, seafaring Vikings invaded France and gained the territory of Normandy. Later, William the Conqueror, Duke of Normandy, invaded England in 1066 and became king of England.

Meanwhile, feudalism had weakened the power of the kings. Under this system, noble lords received royal land in exchange for service to the king. Many of them became more powerful than the king. During the Crusades (1100–1300), many nobles left France to fight for the Catholic Church in the Holy Land.

England and France went to war in 1337 in periodic battles that continued for 116 years, known collectively as the Hundred Years' War. The war was interrupted by a monstrous plague, the Black Death, that killed one-third of all the people in Europe. When fighting resumed, the English nearly conquered the entire country of France. In the end, it was the religious zeal, patriotism and courage of a young girl that altered the course of history.

JOAN OF ARC

Joan of Arc was a shepherdess from the northern village of Domrémy in Lorraine. She claimed that, from the age of 12, she heard voices from God urging her to fight for France. When she was 16, she began bravely to take action.

Joan was determined that the Dauphin, son of the dead King Charles VI, who was disinherited in the Treaty of Troyes in 1420, should still become king of France. She persuaded the young uncrowned king and his leaders that the siege of Orléans would be the battle to end the Hundred Years' War. Dressed in armor, Joan led the newly inspired French troops to victory at Orléans in 1429. She then accompanied the Dauphin to Reims for his coronation as Charles VII.

During the siege of Paris, Joan was captured by the Duke of Burgundy and delivered to the English. When she would not deny that she had heard the saints' voices, she was tried by the Church as a witch and burned at the stake in Rouen in northern France in 1431. She was just 19 years old.

After her death, the spirit of Joan the Maid enabled the French army, believing firmly that God was on their side, to finally drive the English out of France, except for the port of Calais in the far north. Joan revived France's devotion to monarchy. Almost 500 years after her death, in 1920, Joan of Arc was named a saint of the Catholic Church.

THE SUN KING

Louis XIV was the embodiment of absolute power. He controlled the justice system, the military and the nobility. When his prime minister died, he named himself prime minister. He canceled the Edict of Nantes and persecuted the Huguenots, causing many of them to flee France. The loss of their wealth and commercial skills weakened the economy.

Louis built a magnificent palace at Versailles, still one of the glories of all Europe. To his credit, he attracted the most brilliant artists, architects, writers, engineers and scientists of the time to his court. He established himself as the sun, shining his light on those he favored, and so became known as "The Sun King." King Louis XIV was the personification of the quest for glory.

THE RENAISSANCE

During the French Renaissance, much inspiration came from neighboring Italy. New ideas were spread in the writings of Erasmus, Rabelais and Montaigne.

Roughly, the boundaries of modern France were established by around 1500. The greatest flowering of the French Renaissance occurred during the reign of Francis I (1515–47).

Church reform also arrived in the 16th century, inspired by John Calvin. French Protestants, called Huguenots, were persecuted by the Catholics and wars raged for 30 years. Thousands of Huguenots were massacred in Paris in 1572, and thousands more died in the provinces.

The wars ended when the Huguenot leader Henri of Navarre converted to Catholicism and was crowned King Henri IV in 1594. Henri continued to sympathize with the Huguenots and signed the Edict of Nantes in 1598 granting them religious and civil liberties.

The next two kings, Louis XIII and Louis XIV, were both minors when their fathers died. They were trained for leadership by two remarkable, powerful churchmen—Cardinal de Richelieu and Cardinal Mazarin. Through the efforts of these two shrewd tutors, the French throne became an absolute monarchy beginning with Louis XIV (1643–1715).

THE FRENCH REVOLUTION

The seeds of the Revolution wee planted in part by philosophers of the Enlightenment spreading new ideals of justice, and in part by the dissatisfaction of the population with the injustices that existed in society.

King Louis XVI tried to deal with the crisis by assembling the old Estates-General, a body of clergy, nobles and commoners. But the clergy and nobles clashed with the newer class of commoners. This latter group broke away and declared itself a National Assembly.

Thinking that the king was planning to suppress the new assembly, an angry mob stormed the Bastille prison in Paris on July 14, 1789. Soon peasants revolted in the countryside, and fighting erupted in the cities. The French Revolution had begun.

The National Assembly seized control. Traditional privileges were removed from the nobles and clergy, and the feudal system ended.

In 1791, a new constitution changed the absolute monarchy into a constitutional monarchy. The National Assembly divided the country into 83 departments of roughly equal size.

When King Louis and Queen Marie-Antoinette tried to flee the country, they were arrested and forced to sign the new constitution. Royalists throughout Europe tried to restore Louis to his former power. The French revolutionaries declared war against Austria and Prussia. The French Revolution then entered a second, radical phase. Extremist Jacobins under Danton, Marat and Robespierre came to power and set up the Commune of Paris. Massacres and anarchy followed.

In September 1792, the National Convention abolished the monarchy and proclaimed the First French Republic. Louis XVI and Marie-Antoinette were found guilty of treason. The king was guillotined in January 1793. France suddenly found itself at war with all of Europe.

"Men are born and remain free and equal in rights."
— Declaration of the Rights of Man and the Citizen

NAPOLEON BONAPARTE

During the French Revolution, a young officer named Napoleon Bonaparte, born in Corsica, rapidly rose to power. In 1799, Napoleon led a successful coup against the government. He quickly installed a new form of government, the Consulate, with himself as first consul.

Napoleon gave France an enlightened civil code, the Napoleonic Code (1804), and religious tolerance. He created an efficient central government with a stable currency and reasonably just taxes, and founded the Bank of France. He named himself Emperor in 1804, and with his wife Josephine, left a lasting impact on French style and fashion.

A great military strategist and leader, Napoleon proceeded to conquer most of Europe. His troops were finally stopped in Russia by harsh winter weather and a shortage of food. As a result of overexpanding his empire, he lost the throne in 1814. A return to power after exile on the island of Elba lasted 100 days and ended with Napoleon's military defeat at Waterloo in Belgium in 1815.

Napoleon was banished to the island of St. Helena in the Atlantic, where he died in 1821.

The next phase, known as the Reign of Terror, saw a virtual dictatorship of the Committee of Public Safety led by Robespierre. Revolutionary zeal led to the death of 40,000 "enemies of the republic," including Queen Marie-Antoinette, by guillotining and mass drowning. Then Robespierre was arrested and himself guillotined, along with other terrorists.

Another temporary government, the five-man Directory, controlled France from 1795 to 1799. This period saw many elections, revolts and purges, and much general disorder. The end of the French Revolution is marked by the beginning of the French Consulate under Napoleon Bonaparte.

THE SEARCH FOR STABLE GOVERNMENT

After Napoleon's defeat, the Congress of Vienna restored the French borders of 1790. In the years that followed, France underwent several changes in government: it was first an absolute monarchy, then a constitutional monarchy, an unstable republic, an empire and finally a republic as we know it today.

The country was governed by two more Bourbon kings, interrupted by a Second Republic during which all French men got the right to vote. The last king of France, Louis-Philippe, abdicated in 1848. Napoleon Bonaparte's nephew, Louis Napoleon Bonaparte, established the Second Empire and declared himself Emperor Napoleon III in 1852. The Industrial Revolution advanced and new building flourished under this Napoleon, whose reign finally ended with French defeat in the Franco-Prussian War (1870–71).

The postwar treaty forced France to give much of Alsace and Lorraine to the new German Empire. The people ousted Napoleon III and gradually evolved a new constitution which became the basis for the Third Republic. This government lasted until 1940, when the German-backed Vichy government under Marshal Henri Philippe Pétain replaced it during the Nazi occupation of World War II.

France's older colonies in North America, the Caribbean and India were mostly lost or sold by the 1800s. In their place, France established a powerful colonial empire in Africa and Asia. The glory of France was once again exported to new parts of the world: Algeria, Tunisia, Indochina, Senegal, Madagascar, Morocco…

The late 19th century also saw the beginnings of secular, compulsory public education, the growth of the railroads, the rise of labor unions and a clear separation of church and state.

The task facing the Bourbons would have been difficult enough without the problem of finding a stable compromise between those who saw the Revolutionary changes as irreversible and those who were determined to resurrect the old regime.

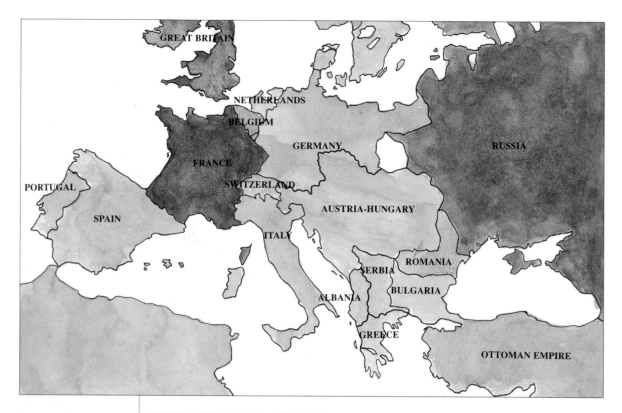

GREAT BRITAIN

NETHERLANDS

BELGIUM

GERMANY

RUSSIA

FRANCE

SWITZERLAND

PORTUGAL

SPAIN

AUSTRIA-HUNGARY

ITALY

ROMANIA

SERBIA

ALBANIA

BULGARIA

GREECE

OTTOMAN EMPIRE

At the beginning of World War I, Europe was divided into two blocs: Triple Entente countries (France, Great Britain and Russia) and their allies versus Triple Alliance countries (Austria-Hungary, Germany and Luxembourg) and their allies. Few nations remained neutral.

TWO WORLD WARS

The first half of this century held much tragedy as well as some glory for France. The great loss of life in World War I, the Depression and defeat by Germany in World War II marked very low periods in French history.

In 1907, France joined with Great Britain and Russia in a diplomatic agreement, the Triple Entente. Germany invaded France shortly after the beginning of World War I (1914–18). Much of the war was fought on French soil, and almost 2 million Frenchmen died. The French soldiers suffered the horrors of trench warfare and of new technologies of death— bombs dropped from airplanes and poison gas.

After the war, Alsace and Lorraine were restored to France, but the French economy had suffered greatly. Recovery depended on German reparations (payments for war losses). In time, Germany stopped paying. During the 1930s, the rise of Fascist leader Adolf Hitler in Germany and the worldwide economic depression led to political turmoil in France.

In September 1939, Germany invaded Poland, touching off World War II, and France joined Great Britain in declaring war on Germany. In May 1940, Germany once again invaded France. France fell quickly, and Germany occupied the northern two-thirds of France, including Paris. Southern France remained in French hands, with a puppet government in Vichy under Marshal Pétain, a World War I hero. In 1942, the Germans also occupied southern France.

In June 1944, American and other Allied soldiers landed in Normandy and liberated France. Pétain was convicted of treason and sentenced to prison for life.

After the war, a new constitution in 1945 created the Fourth Republic led by General Charles de Gaulle. French women voted for the first time that year. France rebuilt its economy with much help from the United States' Marshall Plan. In 1949, France became a charter member of the North Atlantic Treaty Organization (NATO). The Allied victory over Germany ultimately restored France's prewar boundaries.

Some of the heaviest fighting during both world wars took place on French soil.

POSTWAR FRANCE

A referendum to let the French people choose their future government took place in 1945. By an overwhelming majority (95% of the votes cast), the nation rejected a return to the prewar regime. The mood of the liberation era was marked by a thirst for renovation and change.

France lost important colonies after the war. Indochina had been taken by the Japanese during the war, and after the war, France regained control of southern Indochina only. After eight bloody years of struggle, the former colony was divided into Kampuchea (Cambodia), Laos and North and South Vietnam. In 1954, the specter of rebellion reared its head in Algeria, and a long and brutal struggle ensued. Fear that the rebellion would spread to Morocco and Tunisia led the French government to make such drastic concessions to these two countries that they finally gained independence in 1956. The costly war in Algeria lasted through the 1950s, sharply dividing the French people and inspiring terrorist violence. In April 1962, Algeria finally gained independence from France.

The president who succeeded Charles de Gaulle was Georges Pompidou (1969–74), who no longer vetoed Britain's membership in the Common Market. Valéry Giscard d'Estaing, leader of the Independent Republican Party, followed with a coalition government. With the election of François Mitterrand of the Socialist Party in 1981, government ownership of businesses increased.

Socialists also controlled Parliament until 1986, when Jacques Chirac, the conservative mayor of Paris, became prime minister. In 1991, Edith Cresson of the Socialist Party replaced Chirac's successor, Michel Rocard, to become the first woman in French history to hold that post.

The closing decade of the 20th century finds France quite prosperous. Among the problems facing the government, however, are an economic slowdown and the question of how much to support the European single market and unified monetary system beginning in 1992.

As one of the five permanent members of the United Nations Security Council, France maintains a strong position in world affairs.

GENERAL CHARLES DE GAULLE

One of the monumental figures in French history was General Charles de Gaulle. During World War II, he opposed the Nazis and courageously formed a free French government-in-exile in London. His heroic resistance movement spread throughout France.

De Gaulle formed a provisional government after the war and became its president, only to resign in 1946 because he wanted stronger executive powers than the constitution of the Fourth Republic allowed.

De Gaulle returned to power in 1958 and developed a new constitution establishing the Fifth Republic. He was elected to a seven-year term as president. Under this constitution, the powers of the president were greatly increased, while those of Parliament were correspondingly reduced.

De Gaulle worked to make France a strong independent power, free from the domination of either the United States or the Soviet Union. He saw France as the rightful leader of Europe. He recognized the People's Republic of China, encouraged an independent French nuclear-weapons program, and removed all French troops from NATO. De Gaulle urged France to join the European Common Market while keeping Great Britain out.

De Gaulle was a tall, striking man, who seemed in his very person to symbolize French glory. The French people admired his courage and integrity. Yet many eventually began to resent an arrogance that made him seem at times more a king than a president.

De Gaulle's leadership survived student uprisings and widespread strikes that paralyzed the economy. He finally resigned in 1969 after the French people rejected his constitutional reforms. He quietly retired to his country home, where he died the following year.

GOVERNMENT

DEBATING THE BEST FORM OF GOVERNMENT for their country is one of the passions of the French people. They sit at café tables or in the public square and talk endlessly about politics, French leaders and how France could be better governed.

French philosophers and statesmen have struggled nobly with the ideals of good government. Resorting to action rather than words, kings, courtiers, peasants and soldiers of every class engaged in bloody battles over the real power to rule this land. Through the course of its history, France has had many different forms of government including feudalism, absolute monarchy, constitutional monarchy, empire and now parliamentary democracy.

Opposite: **The country town hall may be housed in a charming building with great historical ambience.**

Left: **The Conseil d'Etat is the supreme body consulted by the French government before a new law is passed.**

NATIONAL GOVERNMENT IS STRONG

Until the French Revolution of 1789, France was a monarchy ruled by a king. France is now governed according to its written constitution. The 1958 constitution in use today is the 12th since the revolutionary constitution of 1791.

Today France is a democratic republic, with its capital in Paris. The government of France since 1958 has been known as the Fifth Republic. The president who heads this parliamentary democracy is elected by all voters (citizens aged 18 or older) for a seven-year term. He can be re-elected any number of times. The president appoints the prime minister who then recommends to the president the other ministers who form the Council of Ministers, the French cabinet. The prime minister oversees the day-to-day affairs of the government, while the president, as head of state, focuses more on the direction of national policy and foreign affairs.

In founding the Fifth Republic, Charles de Gaulle greatly increased the actual power of the president. As head of state, the president can dissolve the National Assembly and call for new elections at any time. In an emergency, he can assume almost complete power.

France's national government has three branches. The executive branch is headed by the president and the prime minister. The legislative branch is the Parliament, made up of the two houses—the National Assembly and the Senate. The judicial branch consists of a system of courts. This separation of power into three branches is planned as a system of checks and balances so that no one branch of government can abuse its power.

The National Assembly has 577 members elected for five years by direct universal suffrage. The 319 senators are elected for nine years (one-third every three years) through an indirect system using an electoral college. The Assembly is the more powerful of the two houses.

LOCAL GOVERNMENT

France is divided into 22 regions for planning, budgetary policy and national development. Within the mainland regions are 95 *départements*. Each department has a main town and is run by a general council that includes a commissioner representing the national government and also a local president.

The departments are divided into smaller units called *arrondissements* ("ah-rawn-deez-MAHN"). These in turn are subdivided into "communes," or townships. There are about 36,500 communes in France, ranging in size from small villages to entire cities.

The communes are run by mayors elected by local municipal councils. One of the mayor's duties is to perform marriages.

In France, stability is provided both nationally and locally by a "political class" of men and women whose entire working lives are spent as professionals in government service.

Town halls range from the small functional office to striking architectural marvels, like that of Paris.

The citizens of Paris frequently influence government policies by organizing mass demonstrations along the Champs-Elysées.

BIG GOVERNMENT

The concept of Left and Right in describing political parties stems from the French Revolution. At that time, the radicals sat on the left side of the assembly and the conservatives sat on the right. Today, about five major political parties span the French spectrum from left to right.

On the left are the Socialist Party and the smaller Communist Party. On the right are the Rally for the Republic (RPR), the Union for French Democracy (UDF) and the extremely conservative National Front.

The leftist parties support public ownership or control of most industries. The rightist parties want less government regulation of the economy. The RPR, in the tradition of former French President Charles de Gaulle, favors free enterprise but also a strong national government, a strong military and an independent foreign policy. The National Front (FN) strongly opposes immigration. Labor unions and the Green (ecologist) Party also exert pressure on the government.

In general, French liberals and conservatives today both believe in Big Government. When civic and economic problems arise, most citizens expect the government to take care of them.

CRIME AND PUNISHMENT

France is a civil law country. Cases are decided entirely on the basis of written law. The basis for French law is found in the Napoleonic Code.

Besides the regular court system, there is a separate court system to deal specifically with legal problems of the French administration and its relation to the French citizen. A Constitutional Council rules on constitutional questions.

The French departments have both civil and criminal courts, with courts of appeal for each. Cases involving murder and other serious offenses are heard in courts of assizes. The highest court of the land is the Court of Cassation. Unlike the U.S. Supreme Court, it does not make a final decision. It can criticize legal proceedings and refer a case back to the lower courts to be reconsidered. In France, judges are appointed for life.

A famous image of French punishment has long been the guillotine, a device that cuts off the head of a condemned person. It was adopted during the Revolution as a more humane, quick and painless form of putting a criminal to death than the ways then in use. The man whose name it bears, Dr. Joseph Ignace Guillotin, called it "a cool breath on the back of the neck."

The French tend to be much more lenient in instances of crimes of passion. When it is deemed that a normal person was driven by extreme emotion to commit murder, the penalty is less harsh. It is said that a murderer motivated by passion has never been guillotined in France. In this century, the guillotine has rarely been used, and then mainly to execute the murderers of children, prison guards and kidnap victims. It was last used in France in 1977.

The death penalty was abolished in France in 1981.

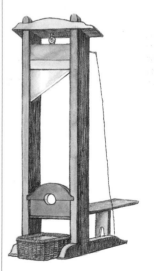

The guillotine has not been used since 1977.

A distinctive feature of the French police is the *képi*, the cap worn by policemen.

ARMED FORCES

The president of France heads its armed forces. Between 16% and 20% of the national budget is spent on the military. Men between the ages of 18 and 35 must serve one year of active duty. About 550,000 men and women are in the army, navy and air force. Those whose beliefs prevent them from fighting must substitute at least two years of public service work.

The *gendarmerie* ("zhawhn-DAHR-muh-REE") serves as militarized state police under the minister of defense, as opposed to the national police force under the minister of the interior.

France is a nuclear power and a major supplier of arms. General Charles de Gaulle, on taking office as president in 1958, said, "There is no corner of the earth where, at any given time, men do not look to us and ask what France has to say." The country's military and foreign policies continue to affect the rest of the world.

The French Foreign Legion is a military corps made up mainly of foreign volunteers paid by France and led by French officers. A legionnaire becomes eligible for French citizenship after serving a five-year period of enlistment with good conduct. The legion was founded in 1831 to help control French colonies in Africa. Members wear a traditional white headdress and take an oath of allegiance to the legion, not to France.

THE FRENCH FLAG

The French flag is called the tricolor because it is divided into three equal vertical stripes of red, white and blue. These colors were first used as a French emblem during the French Revolution. On July 17, 1789, King Louis XVI wore a tricolor knot of ribbons on his hat, combining the colors of Paris—red and blue—with white, the color of the royal family. France has no official coat of arms.

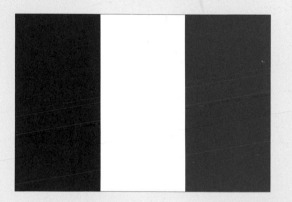

THE LEGION OF HONOR AND OTHER DECORATIONS

The most important existing order that honors outstanding service in France is the Legion of Honor, created by Napoleon Bonaparte in 1802. The Croix de Guerre ("KRWAH duh GEHR") was created to honor the heroic deeds of soldiers who fought in the two world wars. A number of additional civil and military decorations are awarded in France.

ECONOMY

FRANCE TODAY ENJOYS a high level of prosperity. Modernization of French industry began in the early 1950s, and national policy has encouraged a tremendous growth in production and trade since World War II. Huge factories with computers and robots have replaced the typical small prewar manufacturing enterprise. Many workers left the farms to staff the country's growing industrial centers.

France has one of the world's most highly developed economies. It is the third world power in space, after the United States and the Soviet Union. It is first in fast-breeder nuclear reactors and second in offshore oil technology. It has the world's fourth largest economy, with a Gross National Product (GNP) of $956 billion.

The problem of unemployment is reflected in a 1991 rate that hovers around 9% (2.6 million persons out of work, up 1 million from 1981).

Opposite: **The French people prefer to buy their groceries from the neighborhood shop or the street market. They are certain they will get the freshest products.**

Left: **The basic unit of money is the franc which is divided into 100 centimes. Bank notes are illustrated with portraits of famous French men and women.**

France is famed for its dairy products, especially its wide variety of cheeses.

AN ABUNDANCE OF FERTILE SOIL

Of all France's natural resources, the fertile soil is the most vital. A huge portion of the land is fertile, supporting such crops as wheat and sugar beets, fruit orchards, vineyards that generate the fabled wines of France, and grasslands for grazing livestock. Agriculture, including fishing and forestry, accounts for 4% of the GNP.

Acres of forests cover major areas of the French countryside. Their timber is used for building, furniture making and paper making. Though forests are being destroyed at an alarming rate almost everywhere in the world, French forests are actually expanding as a result of careful government planning.

The French have used their land resources wisely. The application of modern farming techniques combined with subsidies given to farmers by the government have helped to make France a leading agricultural producer. Chief products, in addition to those mentioned above, include cattle, milk, potatoes, apples, hogs and chickens. France grows most of its own food and also exports wheat and dairy products.

MINERALS

France has significant deposits of iron ore and bauxite, or aluminum ore. The land also yields coal, gypsum, natural gas, petroleum, potash, salt, sulfur, tungsten and zinc. France is a major producer of uranium, used for nuclear energy and weapons. French ores are used to produce aluminum and steel, which in turn become automobiles and airplanes, industrial machinery, washing machines and refrigerators, and many other products.

THE SERVICE INDUSTRIES

The largest portion of the GNP is devoted to service industries: 62% of the total. Six out of every 10 French workers provide a service. They work in education, health care, trade, banking, hotel and restaurant services, insurance, transportation and communications, and utilities.

About 55.5 million tourists visit France each year. Tourism brings more than $2 billion each year.

France is one of the most popular tourist destinations in Europe. The Sacré-Coeur in Paris attracts tourists all year round.

41

The automobile industry is thriving in France. French-made cars are exported to many distant countries.

FAST TRAINS, FASHION, FOOD AND THE FUTURE

France is one of the most highly developed countries in the world, and industry accounts for 34% of France's GNP, with roughly one out of every three workers employed in industry. The diversified industrial sector includes the production of aircraft, automobiles, chemicals, electronics, food processing, machinery, metallurgy, mining, steel and textiles.

Products that the rest of the world associates with France are often luxury items, such as perfumes, gourmet foods and wines, and dyes and fine fabrics for the fashion industry. But France also exports various products of high technology, such as the world's fastest trains, sophisticated electronics equipment, military airplanes and rockets, and communications satellites. Helicopter-making and shipbuilding continue as important industries.

The automobile industry illustrates the French talent for technical innovation and daring design. French engineers invented the clutch, the gearbox and the transmission shaft, and introduced the front-wheel drive system. Renault and Peugeot-Citroën are leading manufacturers of automobiles that are represented worldwide.

Charming little shops in small towns or villages sell hand-made glassware. The skill is handed down from father to son.

Aircraft manufacture also attracted French design talent with the Caravelle, the supersonic airliner Concorde, the internationally owned Airbus, and the Mystère and Mirage jet fighting planes. Arianespace, the world's leading launcher of commercial satellites, is based in Paris.

Quality and design are exemplified by Michelin tires, Chanel clothing and accessories, Limoges china, Moulinex cooking aids and hundreds of other products for which France is famous around the world.

Though Paris is the center of manufacturing, important factories dot many other regions of the country. Ports and coalfields developed as traditional centers of industry. More recently, the government has given cash and other incentives to promote new small factories in outlying regions.

One surprising aspect of French industry is the manufacture of one particular product—gloves, glassware, copper cookware or knives, for example—in a town or village far from the major industrial centers. Most often, these industries are based on locally available raw materials or a skill that has long been traditional to one family or a small group of people in the region.

Many factories using nuclear and hydro-electric power have sprung up all over France.

ENERGY SOURCES

France's main energy supplies come from imported oil, coal and natural gas, and from domestic hydroelectricity and nuclear power.

Coalfields were exploited for hundreds of years until it became cheaper to import coal from abroad. Because of the shortage of coal reserves, hydraulic power has been harnessed wherever possible, including most waterfalls in the Alps and Jura Mountains, the Pyrenees and the Massif Central, and many rivers.

France is the second-largest producer of nuclear energy for electricity. Nuclear power plants supply more than half of France's electricity, and several new nuclear power stations are opened each year.

The development of nuclear power plants in France stressed safety and economy and thus enjoys more popular support than in countries where serious nuclear accidents have occurred.

People's daily lives are affected by the French policy of energy conservation. Its aim is to lessen French dependence on outside sources of power. Energy-saving plans include reduced speed limits for drivers and limits on home heating levels.

At the mouth of the Rance River on the coast of Brittany, a unique power plant converts the energy of the tides into electricity. Research on alternative power sources such as solar power continues.

TELECOMMUNICATIONS AND TRANSPORTATION

The French have an amazing electronic communications system called Minitel that uses technology for personal convenience. More than 5.5 million telephone subscribers have a computer terminal in their home at no extra charge. They can use it to find phone numbers, make airplane and train reservations, order theater tickets, shop for goods and services, and "talk" via electronic mail. A dating service and about 1,500 videotext services are also available. Customers are charged each time they use the system.

The postal, telephone and telecommunications systems are owned and run by the French government. They receive a huge share of the national budget.

In 1981, the *train à grande vitesse* ("TRAN ah GRAHND vee-TEHS," high-speed train or TGV) began running between Paris and Lyon. In 1989, a still faster version connecting Paris and cities in western France began operation. The TGV can reach a speed of 186 miles per hour, making it the fastest passenger train in the world. But the average speed on daily runs is closer to 162 miles per hour.

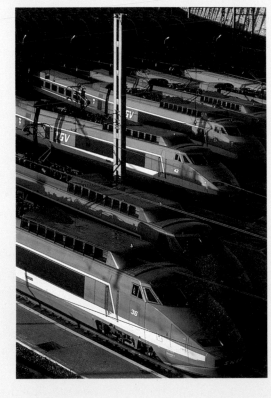

The Paris-Lyon TGV trip is faster than the quickest downtown-to-downtown trip by commercial airline between those cities. For longer routes, however, air travel may still be cheaper and faster.

The TGV system is growing within France and should eventually connect with the Belgian, Dutch, German and Spanish railway systems. Some experts predict the development of still faster trains, with connections all the way to Stockholm in the north and Athens in the south.

Construction began in 1987 on a tunnel beneath the English Channel to link France and Great Britain by rail. Twenty-three of its 31 miles lie under the Channel. When Eurotunnel opens in 1993, high-speed trains will carry passengers from Paris to London in about three hours. Special shuttle trains will carry vehicles and freight.

FOREIGN TRADE AND EUROPE 1992

France is one of the six founder members of the European Economic Community. France and Germany had fought terrible wars three times in 75 years, and it was hoped that if they shared their coal and iron, they would not fight with each other again.

In foreign trade, France ranks behind the United States, Germany, Japan and Great Britain. Its major imports are petroleum products, machinery, agricultural products, chemicals, iron and steel products. Major exports are machinery and transportation equipment including automobiles, airplanes and helicopters, chemicals, agricultural products, iron and steel products, electronic and telecommunications equipment, textiles and clothing, wines and brandies. The value of French imports is slightly larger than that of its exports.

France invests tens of billions of dollars each year in foreign countries, especially former French colonies and other developing countries.

France was a founding member of the European Economic Community, or Common Market, in 1957. Charles de Gaulle had envisioned the EEC as a third great power bloc in the world, inspired by France to remain independent of either the United States or the Soviet Union.

Currently, France trades primarily with other Common Market countries and also with Japan, Saudi Arabia, the Soviet Union and the United States. Within the Common Market, it exports most to Germany, next to Italy, then to Belgium, Luxembourg and Great Britain.

France plans to participate in Project 1992, which will create a single economic area for Europe, similar to the United States. The member countries will enjoy a unified currency, no customs barriers, the relaxation of border controls, no import taxes and other innovations planned to strengthen the European economy.

The success of the 1992 European Community will depend on cooperation among all its members. Yet France is concerned with maintaining its national autonomy and prestige as it becomes more "Europeanized."

FRENCH LUXURIES: PERFUME AND FASHION

The production of perfumes has long been a major industry in France. French perfumes are exported to more than 100 countries.

Since the 1920s, famous fashion designers—Chanel, Yves St. Laurent, Christian Dior, Patou and many others—lent their names to perfumes and reaped fortunes.

Flowers grown in the south, especially around Grasse, have been converted into costly fragrances since the 16th century. Fields of lavender, carnations, lilies of the valley and other flowers brighten the countryside around Grasse.

Today plant oils, animal extracts and less costly synthetic ingredients and chemicals are also prime ingredients in perfumes' closely guarded, secret formulas. These formulas are tested by expert sniffers, mostly men, who are referred to in the business as "noses."

A second industry that links the name of France with elegance, style, quality and luxury is the fashion industry. Other nations have looked to France for creative design of clothing since the 14th century.

In the mid-19th century, an Englishman, Charles Worth, founded the first couture house in Paris. Thus began the modern tradition of marketing fashion to wealthy women from many countries using beautiful models in seasonal fashion shows. New designs are quickly copied in less expensive versions.

French designers and foreign design stars based in Paris influence the look of everything from ballgowns to sportswear, men's clothing, shoes, jewelry and other accessories throughout the western world. True believers in the power of French fashion claim that a silk scarf with the Hermès label can turn any outfit into the epitome of chic.

THE FRENCH

MORE THAN 56 MILLION PEOPLE live in France. The country is so large that it has a relatively low population density—about 268 persons per square mile—when compared to other countries of Europe. The overseas departments and territories contain almost 2 million people.

French people are quite varied in coloring and height, reflecting the country's history as a crossroads of Europe. Early in its history, the region of France was already a melting pot of different tribes, of Mediterranean, Alpine and Nordic types. Gauls, Romans, Germanic tribes and Norsemen carried with them different physical traits and customs.

Opposite: **The beret worn by this old man is a distinctive feature of French dress.**

Below: **Farmers all over the country sport a tanned and rugged look.**

In more recent times, the need for workers brought a wave of immigration from Belgium, Italy and Poland in the mid-19th century. After World War I, immigrants arrived from Algeria, Italy again, Portugal and Spain. Between 1956 and 1976, large numbers of people, both Arabs and Jews, left North Africa to settle in France.

Stereotypes abound. People expect the French from the north to be tall, blond and blue-eyed. Northerners are sometimes perceived as more sophisticated than their southern neighbors, who are expected to be short, with olive skin and dark eyes, more easy-going and slower-paced.

Such generalizations about the French quickly break down. The French are mobile within their borders, like many other populations. Large numbers have moved from village to city and from north to south in the pursuit of jobs and better lifestyles. In addition, 10% of the French (a world record) own second homes, often in regions far removed from their primary household, giving them roots in more than one region of the country.

Still, the diverse French people appear somewhat homogeneous to outsiders. Perhaps what unifies them is the French language and the strong influence exerted by Paris over the rest of the country. Most French people also share the unifying link of their unique history and culture, combined with a fierce love for their country. Writer Christopher Sinclair-Stevenson in his book *When in France* observed accurately: "The French are grumblers, but on one point they are united: France is, for all her faults, the best, most civilized, most beautiful country in the world."

CITY AND COUNTRY PEOPLE

France has at least 57 cities of more than 100,000 people. The largest are Paris, Marseilles, Lyon, Toulouse, Nice, Lille and Bordeaux. During the postwar urbanization of France, Paris doubled in size, while the university town of Grenoble grew rapidly from 80,000 people to more than 400,000. About 74% of the population live in cities and towns, with the remaining 26% in rural areas.

About one-sixth of the total French population live in greater metropolitan Paris. The first Parisians were a tribe of Gauls called the Parisii, who settled an island in the Seine River known as Ile de la Cité ("EEL duh lah see-TAY").

Above: **The Mediterranean type—dark hair and olive complexion—is not restricted to the south. It is now encountered everywhere in France.**

Opposite: **Some villagers supplement their income by selling small amounts of farm produce or dairy products.**

Today, Paris is the capital of French government, business and culture. It sets the trends for the rest of the country in fashion, intellectual life and the arts. It is also one of the most beautiful cities in the world, with elegant restaurants and shops, famous museums and monuments, churches, plazas, boulevards, gardens and parks, and its snaking Seine River. Efficient but less attractive modern housing developments surround Paris to support the city's expanding population.

Other centers of population grew to meet the demands of industry and trade or because of the amenities of resort areas along the Mediterranean Sea and warm, sunny towns in southern France. Most large cities were built near water, on the coast or along inland waterways.

Since the end of World War II, masses of villagers, especially young people, have moved to urban areas in search of better job opportunities and a more comfortable lifestyle. Some villages in poorer regions of the country are now almost deserted. A counter-trend recently has found young people moving back to the countryside to protect France's ecology, enjoy nature, run small businesses and produce crafts outside of the cities.

SOCIAL CLASSES

Though the days of the monarchy and nobility are long past, social classes remain as a remnant of feudal times. The aristocracy maintains its inherited titles and property with great pride. Members live in elegant country *châteaux* and Paris apartments, inviting one another to exclusive parties. However, this class no longer dominates the country as it once did, dictating standards of behavior for all. Increasingly, members of the old aristocracy have intermarried with wealthy members of the middle class.

France has a huge middle class, or bourgeoisie, that virtually runs the country. This class dominates the elite schools and universities. There they receive the special training that prepares them for top jobs in both the public and the private sectors, and make social contacts leading to the best careers. They are doctors, lawyers, teachers, bankers and industrialists, as well as sales executives, skilled technicians and newly rich merchants. Many leading politicians come from this class.

The wealthier and more powerful members of the bourgeoisie make up about 15% of the work force. A larger group—about 40% of the work force—called the *petite* (small) bourgeoisie includes people involved in small and medium-sized businesses, artists and intellectuals, and many office workers.

STRONG REGIONAL IDENTITIES

Regional variations in appearance and customs are most noticeable at the edges of the land. There, certain subgroups within the French population retain distinctive customs, languages, attitudes and even styles of dress that set them apart.

The Bretons express a strong individuality bearing the stamp of their Celtic origins. Regional pride has led many Bretons to retain their ancient language. Breton women wear picturesque white hats, and folk festivals bring forth traditional costumes.

Alsatians share favorite foods, such as sauerkraut, with their German neighbors. The French of Alsace drink more beer than wine and speak a dialect mixed with German.

In southern France, many people in Provence have retained a Provençal dialect influenced by their Roman heritage. The 100,000 Basques have a strange language unrelated to other European tongues and a unique heritage of folklore.

Like the Bretons, the people of Corsica have a strong regional identity. Corsican separatists seeking independence from France have begun to achieve their goals.

The working class—farmers and makers of goods, people who work with their hands—is about 45% of the work force. This class may share lifestyle patterns with the middle class, but they do not advance through the state schools with the same degree of success. In spite of France's ideals of equality, only about 9% of university students come from the working class. A major gap between rich and poor still persists.

More conducive to the ideal of equality is the social welfare system. Rich and poor share equitably in such benefits as maternity care, bonuses for having children, day care for young children, general health and dental care, disability assistance and retirement pensions. About 14% of the people are 65 or older, which places a financial burden on workers to help support those who are retired.

The French are a healthy nation with a low infant mortality rate. The average life span for men is 73 years while for women it is 82 years.

FOREIGNERS ADD SPICE TO THE FRENCH STEW

Immigration has added to the diversity of the French population, at times raising troubling questions about French identity and sparking social tensions. France has about 4 million foreign residents, or 8% of the population. At least half come from North Africa. The rest are from Indochina, Italy, Poland, Portugal, Spain, Turkey, Yugoslavia and other former French colonies.

Large groups of foreigners live in Paris and its environs and in the regions of the Rhône-Alps, Provence and the Riviera. Some 140,000 immigrants have sought political refuge in France in recent years: Chileans, Iranians, Palestinians, Poles and Vietnamese.

About 800,000 French citizens returned from Algeria when it gained independence in 1962. Big settlements of Moslems are concentrated in the port city of Marseilles, where one-sixth of the people now are Arabs. They have both a higher birth rate and a higher level of unemployment than the general population.

France halted the flow of new immigrant labor from developing nations in 1975, but Arabs and Africans continued to arrive through family reunification programs, as political refugees or as illegal immigrants.

France's ultraright National Front Party, headed by Jean-Marie Le Pen, has responded to these new arrivals by encouraging racial intolerance. To counter that influence, a group of students formed SOS Racisme with the slogan *"Touche pas à mon pote!"* ("TOOSH pah ah mohn POHT") meaning "Hands off my buddy!"

Many famous Frenchmen, from designer Pierre Cardin to actor Yves Montand, had foreign parents. Still, each influx of people with different languages and customs causes many French people to debate anew the question, "Who is a foreigner and who is French?"

WHAT IS FRENCH ABOUT THE FRENCH PEOPLE?

A magazine survey revealed in 1988 that the average French man was 5 feet 8 inches tall and weighed 165 pounds, while French women were 5 feet 3 inches tall and weighed 132 pounds. Forty-two percent of the people wore glasses; 86% said they were happy; 96% maintained close relations with their families; 36% smoked; and 45% believed in God.

The French exemplify strong individualism. They love life and the finer things in life: fine foods and wine, the arts and philosophy. They share a conservative respect for tradition and reverence for the past. They take great pride in French products and French style. Many believe in maintaining the purity of their beautiful language.

French people assume they are the best. They like order but hate to be disciplined. They admire logic, cleverness and wit. The French think they are different from the rest of the world, often to the point where they believe foreigners cannot understand them.

On closer inspection, images of the French are varied and often contradictory. In any case, from peasant to aristocrat, the French are like their glorious food—full of flavor and rarely dull.

LIFESTYLE

THE FRENCH PEOPLE have varied customs and traditions. City life is not the same as country life, and different social classes behave in different ways. But *joie de vivre*, a joy in living, is an essential element of every French lifestyle. And *savoir-faire*, the ability to say and do the right thing in any situation, is one of the graces French parents hope to pass on to their children.

Opposite: **One of the joys of retired people is to sit in the park and soak up the rays of the sun.**

Below: **The French love children, and the family unit still forms a strong community.**

FAMILY TIES ARE STRONG

The French cherish family ties. The family is a working unit, a community of interests, leisure pursuits and affection.

In earlier times, a large extended family of grandparents, parents and children all lived together in one household. Today, as customs have changed and the birth rate is relatively low, a typical family is smaller—just the parents and one to three children.

Many children live at home while they attend school and go to a university near their home. When they marry, they tend to settle within about 12 miles of their childhood home.

Families enjoy sharing meals together. They gather around the table to feast together during holidays and important family events. Outsiders are not characteristically included in French family parties. The French guard their privacy.

57

"Sometimes the family is so self-sufficient a society that the Frenchman hardly ventures outside it... It is notorious that he rarely invites non-members of the family to his home: them he meets in a café or a restaurant."
— *Waverley Root*

The French care passionately about their food and drink, and housewives take great care when shopping to seek out fresh ingredients of high quality. They also insist on good value and shop around for the best prices. Traditionally, the French prefer to trade in small family-run shops where they know the owners and enjoy visiting while they make their purchases. They love open-air markets where farmers deliver just-picked fruits, vegetables and flowers.

Close to half of French women now work outside the home, especially in the garment and textile industries and in the retail trade and other service industries. With less time to devote to cooking, they use more convenience foods than in the past and often prefer to shop, minus the social conversation, at large supermarkets where foods are pre-packaged. The still larger "hypermarket" combines the wares of a department store with the supermarket.

The business work day begins early, around 8:00 a.m., and runs to 6:00 p.m. Fathers and children used to come home for a substantial midday meal, but with more mothers working, this practice is growing less common.

In 1982, the official work week was reduced from 40 to 39 hours. In their leisure time, families enjoy gardening, working on home improvements, reading and watching television. Children usually have at least two hours or more of homework during the week, but they, too, enjoy watching television.

Countering the picture of strong family life in France are these trends: marriage and birth rates have fallen in recent years, while the divorce rate has risen considerably. Breaking away from tradition, close to half of young couples living together are unmarried. One out of five babies is born out of wedlock.

RURAL LIFESTYLE

Many rural towns look almost the same as they did hundreds of years ago. In the heart of town is a square bordered by a church, small shops and cafés. Old men play *boules*, and people gossip.

People sit in the cafés, eating and drinking, reading, writing or playing chess. Typical shops include the bakery, the butcher's and the *charcuterie* ("shar-koo-tuh-REE") for cooked meats and sausages. The *tabac* ("tah-BAHK") sells stamps, newspapers and cigarettes. Other small stores sell ice cream and candy, fish, cakes, dairy products, groceries and medicines.

The café is the meeting place for country folk. Here they spend long hours catching up on gossip or discussing politics and current affairs.

Most rural people live in single-story dwellings. Their stone houses have brown, gray or green wooden shutters. Village homes usually have a car, television and modern household appliances.

A typical village will have a belfry tower, a small post and telephone office, a café, one or two restaurants, a town hall with the French flag flying and a grammar school. Many towns have a weekly outdoor market selling fresh produce and sometimes live chickens and rabbits.

Many people in the countryside have never traveled far from their villages. Some still live in homes with dirt floors and no indoor plumbing, maintaining a centuries-old way of life. As farming becomes increasingly modernized, the old peasant farmer is being supplanted by farmers who think and operate more like city businessmen.

CITY LIFESTYLE

The pace of life in cities, especially in Paris, is faster and more hectic than in the countryside. Traffic in the city center is more congested, and the sheer size of the population sometimes makes people more irritable. In the larger cities, most people live in small apartments. The older buildings are often considered the most desirable, with handsome carved moldings and working fireplaces.

Zoning laws protect the center of most French cities, limiting building size and regulating traffic. For that reason, French cities usually have few buildings in the city center that rise higher than eight or nine floors. Handsome rows of trees line the sides of main avenues, while flowers brighten the squares and center strips along main streets. Thousands of workers in green uniforms sweep the streets, keeping them quite clean.

Many young people own a motorbike which they ride to school or to meet friends. Groups of teenagers on bikes near cafés or sidewalks are a common sight.

In the cities, sidewalk cafés are one of the pivots of daily life. People linger here sipping a cup of coffee or a glass of wine, and watch the passing scene. Café owners encourage patrons to stay as long as they wish. Famous writers Jean-Paul Sartre and Simone de Beauvoir wrote their books in a café on Paris' Left Bank, the traditional center of French intellectual and political life.

A particular café may attract mainly writers, artists, musicians or students. Young people flirt in the booths and play jukeboxes and pinball machines in the café but also spend their free time in discos and shopping malls.

City streets tend to be named after famous people, trades and professions, historical events or artists. These names may change with changes in politics.

Ringing the core of cities are burgeoning suburbs, often with massive government housing developments where poorer people can afford to live. More than half the urban population live in new suburban houses or apartment buildings. Suburbanites commute to their jobs on mass transit systems.

Some city dwellers feel their housing is overcrowded and unhealthy. Those who can afford it escape to a second home in the country on weekends or vacations. Many have converted old farmhouses deserted by other families who moved to the city.

People in the cities tend to view country people as old-fashioned, stubbornly adhering to old habits, customs, values and beliefs. On the other hand, they admire country people as the embodiment of hard work, individualism, frugality and common sense. There is a growing nostalgia for the land and the way of life it represents.

French people, particularly young urbanites, are increasingly influenced by trends of modernization and "Americanization." They eat fast-food hamburgers while enjoying American films, television programs and popular music. They love to wear American blue jeans, athletic shoes and baseball jackets and caps. However, even though they imitate the American way of life, they quickly grow out of it and settle into their own culture as they start working.

"It is hard to find a city-dweller in France who has not somewhere in the provinces a parcel of land to which he is strongly attached and to which, very often, it is his dream at last to retire. There is a peasant beneath the surface of every urban Frenchman..."
— *Waverley Root*

CLOTHING REVEALS SOCIAL STATUS AND A VIEW OF LIFE

The French express their role in life through their dress. Blue overalls define a typical worker. Berets are popular in the mountains and among the Basques. Parisian waiters appear in short black jackets or red vests worn with bow ties. Firemen, police and the different branches of the armed forces wear uniforms that are characteristically French.

Young people who belong to successful bourgeois families are called *bon chic bon genre* ("BAWN SHEEK BAWN ZHAHN-ruh"), or BCBG, meaning "good fashion good type" (somewhat like American "preppies"). They wear pastel cashmere sweaters, tweed jackets and silk scarves, and drive BMWs. Denim jeans are also popular. Others wear wilder clothing in styles known as *branché* ("brahn-SHAY"), "punk" and *baba cool*.

Men present themselves as conservative or liberal, traditional or rebellious, depending on whether they choose to wear a suit with tie or to appear tieless, with the suit replaced by a black leather jacket or an old sweater over corduroy pants.

In the villages, men may wear a soft, short-brimmed cap and dark suit jacket, paired perhaps with dark trousers from a different suit. Women appear in flowered dresses, with black sweaters, carrying straw baskets for their grocery shopping. Older widows tend to wear shapeless black dresses with thick black stockings and black shoes.

The French system of education is innovative and goes beyond the classroom. "Snow" or "sea classes," subsidized by the government, enable the students to take advantage of the great outdoors.

EDUCATION

French schools must be doing something right as an impressive 99.2% of adults can read and write.

Schooling is provided free by the government and is compulsory for children between the ages of six and 16. The Ministry of National Education designs the curriculum and the examinations that students must pass. Children between the ages of two and six may attend nursery schools and kindergartens paid for by the government. Reading is taught from age five onward.

Government schools are secular. French families may instead send their children to privately-run religious schools. These schools are mostly Roman Catholic but also Protestant and Jewish. A law from 1959 allows private establishments to sign contracts with the state that procure funds in exchange for some control. About 15% of French children attend primary level private schools, rising to about 23% at the secondary level.

French schools are highly competitive, expecting students to master a wide range of subjects. Discipline tends to be quite strict. In France as elsewhere in the world, the teaching of computer skills has been integrated into the curriculum.

THAT'S TWO "T'S" AND TWO "R'S"

The French are highly literate, yet more then eight out of 10 could not spell the name of their president of 10 years, according to a 1991 survey for *Paris Match* magazine. Eighty-four percent of the more than 1,000 people questioned gave a wrong answer. Only 10% spelled François Mitterrand correctly, and 6% said they did not know. (Many current English language guides to France also misspell "Mitterrand.")

There is relatively little time devoted to after-school activities or inter-school sports competition. Wednesday is a free day when schoolchildren can pursue cultural activities, but students must attend school on Saturday morning. French children have a very long school day (from 9:00 a.m. to 4:30 p.m. with an hour and a half for lunch) but also one of the longest school vacations among European countries.

Secondary school consists of four years of *collège* ("koh-LEHZH") or *lycée* ("lee-SAY"), beginning around age 11. Afterward, some students continue their education at a vocational *lycée* to prepare for a job.

The better students go on to a general *lycée* for three more years to prepare for the baccalaureate exam, the all-important "bac," which they take when they are 18 or older. This exam is so difficult that roughly one-third of the students who take it fail.

Successful candidates for the baccalaureate receive free university education or attend one of the famous *grandes écoles* ("GRAHN-dzay-KOHL"), the elite colleges that train students for the top careers in government service, business, mathematics and engineering.

One of these, L'Ecole Nationale d'Administration (ENA) has been called the most exclusive and prestigious school in France. Its students receive a state salary when they enter and are almost certain that their intense study for two and a half years will lead them to the top in government or politics.

Military academies prepare students for military careers. Family tradition is strong here: eight out of 10 students in these schools are the children of active officers in the French armed forces.

FRENCH WOMEN

French women are perceived to be beautifully dressed and alluring. They are efficient housewives who spend money carefully. In many small family businesses, it is the women who control the cash.

French women did not vote until 1945. Up to 1965, husbands were the legal heads of their families, and women needed their permission to work or get a passport. Husbands managed their wives' money and bank accounts.

Now French women are achieving more equality. Birth control became available in 1967, and in 1975, abortion and also divorce by mutual consent were legalized.

Today women are competing with men for prestigious positions. While the law guarantees women equal pay, French women's average salaries are still far less than those of French men.

Women have long been influential in the French labor movement. As a group, they are taking an increasing interest in politics. They have been elected to Parliament and to municipal councils. In 1991, Edith Cresson became the first woman prime minister of France.

Today's French woman is a free spirit who is still fighting to gain more equality with men in the workplace.

French people shake hands when meeting friends and acquaintances, even if it is for a brief moment in the street.

FRENCH CUSTOMS AND MANNERS

The French shake hands when greeting friends and saying goodbye. Close friends and relatives greet one another with a kiss on each cheek, some southerners adding a third kiss. When a French person enters a room on a social occasion, the newcomer greets everyone in the room.

Traditionally, people call only close friends by their first names, though young people are often more informal about using first names. The French rarely visit someone's home without an invitation. Invitations are usually answered in writing, and thank-you notes are sent soon after a party.

Children generally remain out of sight when their parents have dinner parties at home. Popular gifts to bring to a dinner party are a box of candy, cookies or an odd number of flowers. But a visitor should never bring chrysanthemums, which are associated with funerals. The French do not like to discuss business during social meals.

French Customs and Manners

People greet each other using "Monsieur" ("muh-SYOOR," Mr. or sir), "Madame" ("mah-DAHM," Mrs., madam or ma'am), and "Mademoiselle" ("mahd-mwah-ZEHL," Miss or young lady). They use these terms far more often than English-speaking people do. The French use them generally without adding the person's name. *Bonjour* ("bawn-ZHOOR," hello), *Monsieur*" instead of "Hello, Mr. Jones." The French say hello and goodbye to shop clerks when entering and leaving stores.

Some topics are not considered appropriate for polite conversation: people's age, income, occupation and questions about their family such as how many brothers and sisters they have. Asking how much a personal possession cost or where it was bought is also considered rude, as are talking loudly, gum-chewing in public and calling attention to one's self.

It is sometimes said that the French are careful with money, love a bargain and try to pay as few taxes as possible to the government. Those who dream of becoming instant millionaires may bet at the horse races or buy National Lottery tickets (called Loto) at the corner kiosk.

The French love to argue and debate, to criticize and complain, and they express their true feelings with a gusto that might seem rude to people from other cultures. They tend to be highly critical of both government and business. Although not a nation of "joiners," they sometimes get together for group protests, which occasionally grow into riots or strikes.

The young can be particularly restless, as was illustrated in the student-worker Paris Riots of 1968. Yet there is also in the French people a strong conservative streak that resists change.

French compassion for needy people throughout the world is seen in such groups as the volunteer doctors called Médecins sans Frontières (Doctors without Borders).

"Violent demonstration has been an accepted form of political expression throughout French history."
— The Illustrated Encyclopedia of Mankind

WORKING IN FRANCE

The hours of the day are numbered from one through 24; thus 5:00 p.m. becomes 17:00 hours.

People are expected to be prompt for appointments. Most offices and shops close from noon to 2:00 p.m. Department stores are usually closed on Sunday and Monday.

French workers are entitled to five weeks' vacation a year, and many divide this into three weeks of vacation in the summer and two in the winter. Almost the whole nation goes on vacation at the same time, in the month of August. Paris empties out as people head south, and many stores and restaurants are closed. On the beaches, women in topless bathing suits and even nude bathers are not unusual.

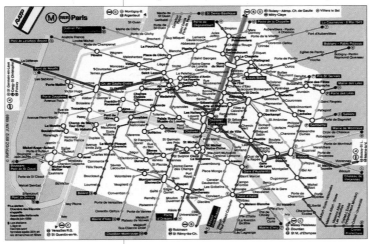

Paris has an efficient _métro_ system criss-crossing the city. Trains are generally clean and punctual.

French cities generally have cheap and dependable bus service, with comfortable trains crossing the country. The Paris subway system is one of the most efficient in the world. On buses and subways, people often give up their seats to senior citizens.

Getting around in cars is somewhat more hazardous, as the French tend to drive faster than official speed limits, aggressively passing slower vehicles. Children are supposed to ride in the back seat of cars. By law, everyone must wear a seat belt when driving on superhighways. It is illegal to honk the car horn in a town. Young people can ride motorized two-wheel mopeds from the age of 14.

THE FRENCH LOVE THEIR DOGS

The well-dressed French woman dining in an elegant restaurant with a French poodle on her lap reflects the national passion for these pets. One French home in three has a dog. People walking in Paris reportedly step in dog droppings every 286th step. It is the city council that cleans up the mess, not the owners.

French thinker Blaise Pascal wrote in the 17th century: "The more I see of man, the more I love my dog." Dogs symbolizing faithfulness were carved on the tombs of French queens. Hunters, including French kings and noblemen, have long idolized their hounds. Napoleon had a favorite poodle named Moustache.

Along with pigs, French dogs—poodles in particular—are used to sniff out the valuable underground truffles so highly prized in French cooking.

German shepherds, wirehaired dachshunds, Yorkshire terriers and red cocker spaniels are among the most popular breeds. French dogs are named for opera characters and figures in ancient history, and also "Rex," "Fifi," "Loulou," "Princesse," "Whisky" and so on. The common dog's nickname "Toutou" is supposed to sound like barking and probably stemmed from the word meaning "you" with which the French address their children—*tu.*

On the outskirts of Paris, a private cemetery for dogs is the final resting place for pets of world-famous and unknown French dog-lovers.

RELIGION

FOR ALMOST 1,000 YEARS of French history, religious differences sparked conflicts and bloody wars. The Roman Catholic religion also inspired the magnificent churches and cathedrals that adorn all parts of France.

France was traditionally Roman Catholic until the French Revolution. In 1789, the state ceased to be officially Catholic. The Concordat of 1804 declared France to be merely "Christian," while in 1905, the law mandated a clear separation of church and state in France. All citizens were guaranteed freedom of religious belief and practice.

The French government recognizes no official church. It is neutral in religious matters and tolerates the peaceful coexistence of different spiritual groups. Religious instruction in state schools is expressly forbidden.

Opposite: **Many Roman Catholic pilgrims from all over the world visit France each year. The pilgrimage to Lourdes is one of the most popular.**

Left: **Although fewer French people today believe in the existence of God, religious fervor is still strong among the millions of believers.**

THE CATHOLIC CHURCH TODAY

Holy Communion is an important step in a person's life. The French celebrate a child's first communion with a special lunch where the whole family gathers together.

Between 75% and 90% of French people consider themselves Roman Catholic, and most have been baptized. But only 14% attend church regularly. Some sections of the country have a much higher percentage of practicing Catholics than others, up to 80% in those rural areas where religious traditions are strongest.

The Catholic Church has its own school system, newspapers, social service organizations and youth groups.

People who rarely go to church may attend during major events in the life cycle. All Catholics are baptized, married and buried by the Church. After a christening, guests and children near the church receive blue or pink candy-coated almonds called *dragées* ("drah-ZHAY"). A special ceremony is held when children take Communion and receive Confirmation at around age 11 or 12. For Holy Communion, the children wear white with an additional white veil for the girls. They may receive a gift, such as a prayerbook, bound in white. At the family celebration, only white food is served.

Critics of the conservatism of the Catholic Church claim that its rigid, traditional viewpoint has made it harder for the French people to make the necessary adjustments to modern life.

In any case, the influence of the Catholic Church over the French people has diminished greatly. Fewer men choose to become priests. Many people ignore Catholic doctrine forbidding divorce and abortion.

Recognizing a need for change, the Catholic Church has tried to reach out to more people, adapting to the needs of modern lifestyles without losing the traditions of the past. The prayer services have been simplified. Masses are now conducted in French rather than the traditional Latin.

The church has stepped up its involvement in progressive social action. Some worker-priests hold ordinary jobs and try to share the lives of the working class. An ecumenical outreach to non-Catholic Christians and to people of other religions marks the new attitude of the French Catholic Church.

Some conservative Catholic leaders, led by the far-right former archbishop Monseigneur Lefebvre, have reacted strongly against these liberalizing trends in the church. About 10% of Catholics support a return to old-fashioned discipline and strict observance of church doctrines.

Catholic priests are now taking on a more varied social role in order to reach out to more people.

PROTESTANTS IN FRANCE

Minority religions represent a small fraction of the population. Protestants were once spread throughout France, but the 16th-century Wars of Religion and the revocation of the Edict of Nantes in 1685 greatly curbed the power of these Huguenots. Many children born of Protestant parents did not have any civil status as Catholic priests, who were the only ones authorized to conduct marriage services, refused to officiate at Protestant weddings. It was not until 1787 that an edict gave them back their civil rights. Freedom of worship was granted during the Revolution.

The leading early Protestant associated with France was Jean Calvin (1509–64). He was born in France and educated at the University of Paris. In 1533, he moved to Switzerland to avoid persecution as a Protestant. He taught that God decided before people were born who would be saved— that is, salvation by predestination.

Today, about 2% of the French are Protestant, belonging to several different denominations. The leading one is the Reformed Church of France. Activities of all the Protestant churches are coordinated by the Protestant Federation of France, founded in 1905. Protestants live primarily in Paris, parts of Alsace, the Jura, the Massif Central and the central Atlantic regions. They are active in French business and politics, with at least five having attained the post of prime minister.

OTHER RELIGIONS

With about 3 million believers, Islam is the second religion in France. The Moslem population includes many recent immigrants from North Africa and makes up about 3% of the population. Moslems have settled especially in Marseilles and the immigrant neighborhoods of Paris.

There are more Jews living in France than in any other Western European country. About 1% of the French people are Jewish. Half live in and around Paris, a quarter in Marseilles, and many in the larger towns in the east and in the Alsace region.

Anti-Semitic sentiments in the 7th and 14th centuries led to the expulsion of thousands of French Jews. Later, they endured deportations to death camps during World War II when France was occupied by Nazi Germany.

Still, Jewish life thrives, marked by flourishing kosher restaurants, Hebrew schools and synagogues. Jewish children are usually given names from the standard lists of names of the saints, but their last names often reveal their heritage. Anti-Semitism occasionally surfaces in France, in neo-Nazi and Arab attacks on Jewish people and their synagogues, businesses and cemeteries.

Small immigrant groups also practice Hindu, Buddhist and other religions. Cults such as Moonies and Hare Krishna have not gained a large following. Freemasons have a long history in France. They participate actively in politics, with a tendency to "leftist" views. About 6% of the people declare themselves unaffiliated to any religion.

RELIGION INFLUENCES FIRST NAMES

Since 1539, parents have been legally required to register their children's names. Until the Revolution, babies had to be named after a Catholic saint. In addition to birthday celebrations, the French people sometimes also have a party on their Name Day, the feast day of the saint after whom they are named. Even non-Catholics tend to give their children first names of Catholic saints. With certain exceptions, French citizens cannot legally change their names as registered at birth.

Popular first names in recent years have included André, Claude, Jacques, Jean, Michel, Pierre and René for boys, and Brigitte, Danielle, Jeannine, Marie, Martine and Sylvie for girls. Double first names, such as Jean-Pierre or Marie-Christine, are also very popular with young parents.

MIRACLE AT LOURDES

Devout Catholics make pilgrimages to sites where they believe miracles occurred. One much-visited shrine is in Lourdes in southwest France. There, Bernadette Subirous, a 14-year-old girl, said that the Virgin Mary appeared to her in 1858. She had 18 visions. In the grotto where she saw the Virgin, Bernadette scratched the dry ground with her fingers. A gush of water came forth where no spring had existed before. The water seemed to have healing powers.

Church officials were skeptical, but four years later, after much inquiry, Rome declared these events miraculous. In 1933, the Church named Bernadette a saint. The world's largest underground church, capable of holding 20,000 people, was built to mark the 100th anniversary of the miracle at Lourdes.

More than 3 million pilgrims visit Lourdes each year, with the largest of six yearly pilgrimages on August 15 (Assumption Day). People light candles and kneel to express their faith. They pray to the Virgin to cure their ills and handicaps. Discarded crutches are stacked at the entrance to the Cave of Apparitions.

The health of the local economy also benefits from the miracle. Lourdes has the largest number of hotel rooms of any French city except Paris. Souvenir shops sell plastic bottles in the shape of the Virgin, filled with the holy water.

LANGUAGE

ONE OF THE JEWELS OF FRANCE is its official language, French. This precise and beautiful tongue has been a major factor in unifying the diverse peoples who settled France. The French language has carried the glorious achievements of French culture around the world.

A LANGUAGE OF CLARITY AND BEAUTY

From the mid-17th century to 1920, European intellectuals and leaders preferred French to their native tongues. French thrived as a language of diplomacy and is today one of the two languages, along with English, in which all United Nations documents are published.

French is also an official language of Belgium, Canada, French Guiana, Haiti, Luxembourg, Monaco and Switzerland. It is the official language of the French overseas departments and one of the official tongues in many former French colonies.

French is still an important tongue in Cambodia, Laos, Vietnam, Lebanon, Syria, Jordan and Iran. More than 90 million people use French as their first language, and millions more speak it as a second language.

The governments of French-speaking countries created an organization in 1986 called La Francophonie. Its members wrestle with world problems, agriculture, scientific research and other areas of mutual concern.

Opposite: **Shops and cafés in France display charming signs. This one advertises the "products of Norman soil."**

Below: **The French are very proud of their language which is perceived as a language of refinement.**

MODERN FRENCH HAS MANY SOURCES

Regional dialects, some older than the French language, are still spoken in various parts of the country.

Along with Italian, Spanish, Portuguese and Rumanian, French belongs to the family of Romance languages. These evolved from the Latin tongue used by the Roman conquerors. The people in the region of modern France spoke a Celtic language known as Gaulish when the Romans conquered them. About 350 words in modern French can be traced to Gaulish.

The Frankish invasion contributed about 1,000 words to modern French, along with the name of the country. Danish Vikings added roughly 90 words. During the Renaissance, many words came into the language from Latin and Greek. Neighbors Italy and Spain also contributed many words to French.

Old French was spoken from the 9th to the 14th century. It had two main dialects—*langue d'oc* ("LAHNG DOHK") in the south and *langue d'oïl* ("LAHNG DOY") in the north. *Oc* and *oïl* were the words used to mean "yes." The northern dialect became the language of the country because Paris was so influential. The dialect of the south survives in the regional dialect called Provençal.

Charlemagne as early as 813 distinguished between the "rustic Romance tongue" and the "Latin tongue" and proposed the use of the former in church services. The first known written document in French was the Oaths of Strasbourg, a treaty signed in 842. It was not until the 16th century, however, that French totally replaced Latin as the language for official documents.

Regional dialects are still spoken, especially at the edges of the country. They include Alsatian, Basque, Breton, Catalan, Flemish and Provençal. As some dialects have diminished in importance, French scholars have grown increasingly interested in studying and preserving them.

THE ACADÉMIE FRANÇAISE

"It is a tradition solidly established in France to see in the purity of the language the image of the grandeur of the state." —linguist Claude Hagège

The official guardian of the purity of the French language, the Académie Française, was founded in 1635 by Cardinal de Richelieu. His goal was to make French a universal language like Latin and to make it both clear and stable. He succeeded so well that French is particularly praised for the clear meaning of words and logical rules of grammar. These virtues are also great assets in conducting international business and diplomacy.

There are 40 Academy members, known as the "40 immortals." They are chosen from among France's leading writers, scientists, statesmen, military leaders, lawyers and churchmen. The first woman was elected in 1980.

Members meet weekly, and they serve for life. They do this with great style, as they are initiated wearing ceremonial swords, cocked hats and elaborate uniforms embroidered with green palms.

Their main task is to write and edit the Dictionary of the French Academy, the ultimate authority on all questions concerning the French language. The Academy's work has discouraged rapid changes in the language, enabling modern readers to understand easily French literature written many centuries ago.

The Academy particularly resists adopting foreign words into French. After World War II, more than 2,000 English words entered the French language— words like *le weekend, le drugstore, le hamburger.*

BODY LANGUAGE

You can tell whether people are French just by watching them talk. The French use their entire faces to emphasize what they are saying—eyebrows rise, foreheads wrinkle, broad smiles appear. Lips purse to form the vowel sounds. The hands are always moving, especially among people in the south.

French body language is fairly easy to understand. The shoulder shrug means "I don't know," "I don't care," or "There's nothing I can do about it." Two outstretched hands, palms up and fingers spread, can mean helplessness, anger or indifference. A circle made of thumb and forefinger with the other three fingers raised means "O.K." or, better yet, "perfect."

KEEPING THE LANGUAGE PURE

Both the French educational system and the conservative Académie Française help to standardize the usage and pronunciation of French words throughout the country. Thus, people from all parts of France and of every social class can easily understand one another.

In the 1970s, the French government outlawed the use of any foreign word in official documents, on radio and television, and in advertising, if an equivalent French word already existed. Officially, the French view the English words cropping up in their language as an invasion sure to have disastrous consequences.

Unofficially, younger and more casual French people like the flexibility they gain from English words and phrases. As writer Carl Bernstein observed, it is easy to combine words into catchy new expressions in English but almost impossible in French.

In matters of language, France has exported at least as much as it imported. English has borrowed words from French since the Norman Conquest of England in 1066. It is estimated that 40% to 45% of all English words have French origins. Borrowed words reflect everything from religion—"pray," "saint," "faith"—to French leadership in fashion and food—"chic," "gourmet" and "vogue." French also lent countless words to the other European languages and, to a lesser extent, to languages in Asia and Africa.

In 1991, the government decreed many radical spelling changes involving plural forms, hyphens (*le blue-jean* became *le bluejean*) and accent marks. The Académie Française at first approved the changes but later the members changed their minds and rejected the reforms. Many French writers organized to resist the changes, but there is a precedent for such rules imposed from on high. In 1740, the Académie Française itself decreed spelling changes for one-quarter of the words then in use.

PROVERBS WITH A FRENCH TWIST

Similar proverbs take on a different flavor in a different language. Compare these English proverbs and the English translation of the French version:
English: Too many cooks spoil the broth.
French: Too many cooks ruin the sauce.
English: Don't count your chickens before they're hatched.
French: Don't sell the bearskin before you kill the bear.
English: You cannot make a silk purse out of a sow's ear.
French: There's no way to turn a buzzard into a hawk.
English: Little drops of water make the mighty ocean.
French: Little by little the bird makes its nest.

Magazine publishing is a flourishing industry in France. There are magazines for all kinds of tastes and interests.

THE PRESS

Freedom of the French press is guaranteed in principle by the Declaration of the Rights of Man. Since 1939, the number of daily newspapers published in France has shrunk from 220 to 82. Of these, 12 come from Paris and 70 from the provinces. Leading newspapers published in Paris include the liberal *Le Monde* (The World), the conservative *Le Figaro*, and also *France-Soir* and *Le Parisien Libéré*.

At the same time, publishing has spread from its original concentration in Paris to the provinces. The avid French reader can sit in cafés throughout France poring over international, national, regional and local news, and getting a wide range of political opinions. The regional paper with the widest circulation is *Ouest-France* (West France), published in Brittany's capital of Rennes.

Magazine publishing has mushroomed, with the emergence of special-interest magazines covering the youth market, sports, women's concerns, business, the media, religion, home improvement, health, the arts and sciences, and, of course, the news. *Paris Match* features photojournalism and is the most popular magazine in the news category. More popular still is the TV weekly *Télé 7 Jours* ("tay-lay set ZHOOR," TV 7 Days), with more than 3 million readers.

Of the French-based international news agencies, the largest is L'Agence France-Presse (A.F.P.), founded in 1944 and operating in more than 100 countries around the world.

RADIO AND TELEVISION

The French government administers Radio France's five local stations and Radio France International's numerous stations, reaching an estimated potential audience of 80 million listeners worldwide. In addition, some 1,800 private local radio stations broadcast round-the-clock programs over FM frequencies. Near the borders, French audiences can pick up both radio and television broadcasts from neighboring Luxembourg and Monte Carlo, and other foreign countries.

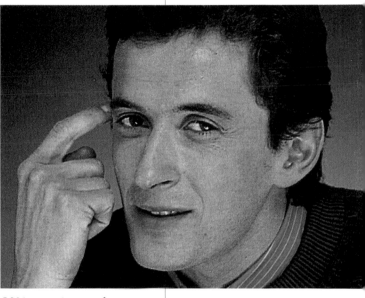

Almost every French home has at least one radio. Ninety-five percent of French households also have television, with about 80% owning color sets. Radio and television broadcasts reach the remotest areas of the country as France has one of the most advanced and efficient telecommunications systems in the world.

Christophe Dechavanne is one of the most famous TV entertainers in the country. A number of radio and television personalities have attained star status.

Of the six French television channels, two are public service channels, and four are privately-run. A seventh cultural channel offers joint French and German programming. About half of all TV programs shown on French television are imported from other countries, especially the United States. French viewers enjoy watching American-style soap operas and action films.

French television focuses so often on interviews with leading politicians that they tend to become media celebrities. The government maintains an interest in upholding the educational and cultural level of French television and resisting American influences.

ARTS

THE ARTS HAVE FLOURISHED IN FRANCE for thousands of years. Prehistoric drawings almost 20,000 years old adorn the walls of the famous caves of Lascaux in southwestern France. The country itself is an outdoor museum of great styles of architecture, with very old buildings often standing right next to controversial new ones.

THE GLORIES OF FRENCH ARCHITECTURE

Decorated prehistoric caves and Celtic graves containing jewelry and helmets are evidence of the earliest settlers. Roman civilization left marvels of construction—aqueducts, amphitheaters and scattered ruins throughout the country. In the Middle Ages, romanesque churches, abbeys and castles were built in a heavy and solid style, with round arches and flattened columns.

The Gothic style, from the mid-12th through the 15th century, makes use of pointed arches, ribbed ceiling vaults, colorful stained-glass windows, delicate spires reaching to the heavens, and elaborate decoration with religious statues. Flying buttresses that link the outer walls to free-standing columns were first used at Notre-Dame Cathedral in Paris, built from 1163 to 1330. The medieval abbey of Mont-Saint-Michel, built over several centuries, has aspects of both Romanesque and Gothic styles.

Renaissance architecture in the 16th and 17th centuries revived classical forms such as the Roman arch, dome and Corinthian columns. Renaissance buildings, including Fontainebleau palace outside Paris, are harmonious and symmetrical.

Opposite: **The grand staircase of the Paris Opera is a marvelous example of French art and architecture.**

Below: **Juxtaposition of modern and classical architecture at the Louvre, one of the most famous museums in the world.**

THE EIFFEL TOWER

A symbol of Paris since it was built for France's Centennial Exposition of 1889, the striking Eiffel Tower was the tallest building in the world until 1930. Its construction of lacy wrought iron was a technological breakthrough, engineered by bridge builder Alexandre Gustave Eiffel.

The revolutionary height and arresting design provoked great controversy 100 years ago. The tower was almost demolished in 1909 but was saved to house transmitters for the first transatlantic wireless telephones. Today, the Eiffel Tower holds radio and television transmitters, three restaurants, a post office and a steady stream of visitors who ride to the top for a dazzling view over Paris.

The baroque period that followed brought an integration of the building with elaborate gardens with lakes, fountains, clipped trees and hedges, and flowerbeds laid out in formal patterns, as in the Tuileries and at Versailles. A distinctive feature of French buildings, the sloping mansard roof, appeared at this time—the creation of François Mansart.

Succeeding styles—rococo, neo-classical, Art Nouveau, art deco—reflected the changing lifestyles of the French people and the new technologies available to builders. Emphasis shifted from buildings for the Church, kings and nobles to structures for the public.

The beauty of Paris has been preserved by Baron Haussman's 19th-century plan for the city based on buildings of a maximum height of seven stories. Skyscrapers, except one, are far from the center. In the rest of France, most regions have distinctive architectural details, with building materials and roof styles giving each town a particular charm.

Today French architecture has an international flavor. Three Paris museums are among the most noteworthy architectural projects of the 20th century, and all used foreign architects.

The Louvre has been under construction, on and off, since the 13th century. It provides a unique showcase for the history of French architecture. More recently a controversial new entrance was built: a 71-foot high glass pyramid placed in the historic palace courtyard.

CHÂTEAUX AND PALACES

Castles, or *châteaux*, are among the most beautiful examples of French Renaissance architecture. A string of beautiful *châteaux* stretches along the valley of the Loire River. Some of the finest are at Blois, Chambord, Cheverny, Amboise, Chaumont and Chenonceaux. Most were built and redesigned over several centuries.

Here religious conflicts and quarrels over succession to the throne sometimes led to murder and revenge. Here, too, French culture blossomed during the Renaissance.

Many are still filled with elegant antique furnishings, paintings and tapestries, and are surrounded by glorious gardens. The *château* at Chambord, with 365 chimneys, contains 440 rooms and 85 staircases. It was the site of the world's first sound and light show.

Another sound and light show illuminates the colorful history of the *château* of Chenonceaux, which belonged in turn to King Henri II, his favorite mistress, Diane de Poitiers, and his wife, Catherine de Médicis. The *château* of Ussé looks like the castles of fairy tales and is said to have inspired the story of *Sleeping Beauty*.

Near Paris, the spectacular palaces of Versailles and Fontainebleau functioned as hunting lodges and as homes for royalty and their retinue of thousands of nobles, servants, artists and soldiers. Napoleon Bonaparte signed his abdication at Fontainebleau. The many important historical events that occurred at Versailles span the beginnings of the French Revolution to the signing in its Hall of Mirrors of the Treaty of Versailles at the end of World War I by the Allies and Germany (1919).

The National Museum of Modern Art in Paris houses masterpieces of modern art, such as Matisse's *Large Red Interior* painted in 1948.

FRENCH VISUAL ARTS ILLUMINATE OUR WORLD

The first paintings in France were the work of Cro-Magnon cave-dwellers. They drew wild animals on the walls of their caves—reindeer, horses and bisons—perhaps hoping for magical assistance in the hunt.

Manuscript illumination flourished in the Middle Ages. But the real emergence of a French school of painting occurred during the 17th century. Leading Baroque artists included Georges de La Tour and the Le Nain brothers. Claude Lorrain and Nicolas Poussin were masters of landscape painting. Charles Le Brun was court painter to Louis XIV and the decorator of opulent Versailles.

In the 18th century, Antoine Watteau, François Boucher and Jean-Honoré Fragonard were leading court artists who celebrated the theater and light-hearted beauty and romance, while Jean-Baptiste-Siméon Chardin became known for simpler domestic scenes and still lifes.

Jacques-Louis David, court painter to Louis XVI, was the prime illustrator of the Revolution and the Napoleonic era. Romantic painter Eugène Delacroix's *Liberty Leading the People* was inspired by Revolutionary events.

Honoré Daumier's sharply witty, satiric work portrayed the professional classes. Camille Corot, Jean-François Millet, the realistic painter of peasants, and Gustave Courbet, another realist, created enduring masterpieces.

For the next century, most important art movements began in Paris. Some of the most noted artists working in France were of foreign birth—Vincent Van Gogh, Pablo Picasso, Amadeo Modigliani and Marc Chagall.

French Visual Arts Illuminate Our World

Anyone who wishes to become familiar with French painting could begin by studying the work of Georges Braque, Paul Cézanne, Salvador Dali, Edgar Degas, Paul Gauguin, Edouard Manet, Henri Matisse, Claude Monet, Pierre-Auguste Renoir, Henri Rousseau or Henri de Toulouse-Lautrec. They have left vivid images of the people, landscape, food and flowers of France. They also explored new ways to paint light and shadow, color and space.

Revolutionary art movements in France developed in stunning succession: Impressionism, Expressionism, Symbolism, Fauvism, Cubism, Dada and Surrealism. Through their handling of line and color, painters expressed their personal emotions, dreams and subconscious impulses or their cooler intellectual concerns.

Twentieth-century painters Balthus, Alberto Giacometti, Jean Dubuffet, Yves Klein, Victor Vasarely and others turned out innovative masterpieces that enrich museum collections in the major cities of the world. But it is perhaps Matisse and Picasso who will be best remembered as the great French artists of this century for their long, creative lifespans during which they produced a stunning array of artworks in varied styles.

Traditionally, French painters also applied their talents to sculpture, ceramics, collage, weaving and tapestry, and other decorative arts. Museums proudly display the sculptures of Degas, Giacometti, Dubuffet, Aristide Maillol, Jean Arp, Matisse, Picasso and many others. Probably France's foremost sculptor was Auguste Rodin (1840–1919), whose works *The Thinker* and *The Kiss* are two of the best-known in the world.

The visual arts reach the public in many guises. American writer Richard Bernstein singled out the comic strip as the most popular cultural form in France. Called the *bande dessinée* ("BAHND deh-see-NAY"), or B.D. for short, the graphic designs, notes Bernstein, "break new ground in every issue." This art form enjoys a huge, devoted following.

The Marsupilami is a fantastic animal whose adventures are told in B.D. form.

FRENCH IMPRESSIONISM

French Impressionism is so widely loved today that it is hard to imagine the fury it provoked when its artists first showed their work in Paris. The appearance of Edouard Manet's *Luncheon on the Grass* in an 1863 exhibition touched off the revolutionary new art movement.

It was Claude Monet who gave the movement its name, from his 1872 *Impression, Sunrise*. The Impressionists organized eight of their own exhibitions in the 1870s and 1880s. The artists included Monet, Sisley, Pissarro, Renoir and Degas. Although the interests and styles of the individual artists differed, they cooperated in showing their work and greatly influenced one another.

The Impressionists stressed color and composition over story content, emotions and symbols. They worked outdoors, used small canvases and made freer brushstrokes to capture the quickly changing atmosphere. Collectors delight in the Impressionist images of light and color, sunny landscapes and shimmering water.

Among the most fascinating Impressionist paintings are Monet's series of pictures of poplar trees, haystacks, water lilies and Rouen Cathedral. He painted the same scenes at different times of the day, trying to capture the fleeting effects of light on the ever-changing natural world.

Renoir was known for sensuous, colorful pictures of pretty women and children and joyous crowd scenes. Degas portrayed bathers and dancers.

An assortment of styles and subjects characterized the many great Post-Impressionist artists who followed: Toulouse-Lautrec's Moulin Rouge cabaret dancers, Cézanne's landscapes that so greatly influenced cubism, Gauguin's exotic scenes of South Sea Islanders, and Van Gogh's colorful, often tortured still lifes and portraits. Van Gogh and Gauguin moved beyond Impressionism to use color for its emotional, expressive and decorative elements.

After a long struggle for recognition, Impressionist and Post-Impressionist paintings received great critical approval and now sell for very high prices.

LITERATURE OF IDEAS AND PASSION

French literature has vitally affected politics. Philosophy, religion and theater have attracted some of the greatest writers. The ideas of the writers have in turn sparked riots, revolution and reform.

Of the poetry and love songs of the medieval French writers, the best-known are *The Romance of the Rose* and *The Song of Roland* (about 1100), an epic based on the defeat of Charlemagne at Roncevaux in 778.

A great French work still read today is *Gargantua* and its sequel, *Pantagruel,* by Renaissance writer and humanist François Rabelais, who gave the term "Rabelaisian" to his style of earthy humor.

The classical age was a high point in French literature, especially during the reign of Louis XIV. In the 17th and 18th centuries, great classical playwrights Pierre Corneille and Jean Racine wrote tragedies, while Molière wrote comedies poking fun at human frailty.

French was the language of the educated classes of all Europe, and French arts and literature were widely admired. The mathematician and creator of analytic geometry René Descartes pronounced the famous words, "I think, therefore I am" and thus inspired modern philosophy.

Eighteenth-century Enlightenment writers included the brilliant and prolific Voltaire. He opposed intolerance and prejudice and wrote a work banned for its attack on the French regime and also a famous novel, *Candide*. Denis Diderot devoted much of his life to creating a great French encyclopedia.

A Romantic reaction against the Age of Reason led to the glorification of emotion and imagination. Swiss-born Jean-Jacques Rousseau's *The Social Contract* argued that people are by nature happy and good, but that government and society are the cause of their troubles. Rousseau is said to have inspired the outbreak of the French Revolution.

"An invasion of armies can be resisted, but not an idea whose time has come."
— *Victor Hugo*

93

One of the most famous women writers in France is George Sand who wrote various novels, short stories and letters for adults and children.

Poet, playwright and novelist Victor Hugo was a leading Romantic writer. Author of *The Hunchback of Notre Dame*, his *Les Misérables* portrayed incidents of the Revolution and was a plea for social justice.

The adventurous stories *The Three Musketeers* and *The Count of Monte Cristo* by Alexandre Dumas are still enjoyed by young people around the world. Jules Verne's novels were the forerunners of modern science fiction. A more recent favorite of younger readers is Antoine de Saint-Exupéry's fable, *The Little Prince*.

Gustave Flaubert wrote his famous *Madame Bovary* in a realistic style. Emile Zola carried realism even further in a style called naturalism, exploring the squalid lives of the poor. Anatole France wrote novels about the Revolution and won the Nobel Prize in 1921.

In the early 1900s, Marcel Proust wrote his epic *Remembrance of Things Past*, which many people consider the greatest modern French novel and one of the finest books of all time.

André Gide won the Nobel Prize in 1947 and raised ideas that led into the French Existentialism of the World War II period. Jean-Paul Sartre and Algerian-born Albert Camus developed these ideas of free will and moral responsibility in their novels and plays, and each won a Nobel prize, though Sartre turned his down in 1964.

More recent writers of note include Alain Robbe-Grillet, Claude Simon, who won the Nobel Prize in 1985, Marguerite Duras, who also wrote filmscripts, Marguerite Yourcenar and Michel Butor. Theater of the Absurd attracted the great talent of Irish playwright Samuel Beckett, who wrote in both French and English.

One of the best-loved French literary characters is Babar the elephant, created by father and son Jean and Laurent de Brunhoff. The stories have delighted children for over half a century.

FRENCH MUSIC

French music continues to delight audiences around the world. Georges Bizet's opera *Carmen* and Maurice Ravel's *Bolero* are well-known from live performances and recordings but also as background music to Olympic skating competitions and lusty Hollywood films.

Until the 19th century, France imported more music than it created. Early French composers of note were François Couperin and Jean Philippe Rameau in the 18th century.

The French appreciate originality and experimentation in music as in the other arts. Hector Berlioz and Claude Debussy were pioneers whose influence in music mirrored the revolutionary contributions of French painters of their time. Debussy's subtle tonal shadings and the sense of painting a picture with sound gave his music the name of "impressionism."

A leading 20th-century innovator, composer-conductor Pierre Boulez created music in the 12-tone scale and also blended tape recordings with live music in a form called "concrete music." Pierre Schaeffer, a French engineer, invented the technique of "concrete music."

Olivier Messiaen introduced into Western music unfamiliar modes from the Middle Ages, rhythms from India, sounds from nature—especially the songs of birds—and tried to express his fervent Catholic religious faith through music.

Paris enjoyed one of the world's first modern symphony orchestras. Music was added to the official school curriculum in the 1970s. Today, municipal opera houses are found in many of the large cities.

Regional music festivals flourish, especially in the south. All forms of music, from chamber music to jazz, have their stars and their enthusiastic French fans. The more than 25,000 rock groups attract tremendous support, especially from teenagers.

Although we tend to think of architecture, painting and literature as the pre-eminent French arts, French music is appreciated by people all over the world.

The Moulin Rouge is most famous for its French cancan shows and cabaret revues.

MINUET, CANCAN AND BALLET

The minuet was performed by aristocratic couples from about 1650 to 1750. Ballet came to France from Italy and flourished from the 16th century. Its popularity later diminished but was revived by the dazzling performances of the Ballet Russe in Paris headed by Serge de Diaghilev.

Popular 19th-century French ballets include *La Sylphide* and *Giselle*. Marius Petipa created the immensely popular *Sleeping Beauty* and *The Nutcracker*. He also developed the vocabulary and techniques that defined classical ballet after his time.

Known for its high kicks that showed the petticoat and legs of the women dancers, the cancan grew popular in Paris dancehalls in the 1830s. The music of Jacques Offenbach's *Gaîté Parisienne* is linked with this quintessentially French dance style.

American black artiste Josephine Baker became famous in Paris for her spirited dancing in *The Black Revue* and for her habit of strolling the Champs-Elysées with a diamond-collared pet leopard.

Today, many ballet companies thrive in Paris and the provinces. Known internationally are the innovative Ballet of Maurice Béjart and the prestigious ballet company of the Paris Opera.

Although the French film industry produces more than 100 films a year, movie-goers also appreciate foreign films dubbed in French.

FILMS

The French were the major pioneers in film-making in the 1890s. The French "new wave" films of the 1950s gave greater importance to the personal vision of the director than to the screenwriter or featured actors.

Early outstanding directors included Marcel Carné, René Clair, Jean Renoir and Jean Cocteau. New wave directors included François Truffaut, Jean-Luc Godard, Eric Rohmer and Claude Chabrol. The new wave crested in mid-century, and more recently a different viewpoint has been expressed by directors Louis Malle and Bertrand Tavernier.

Landmark French films include Roger Vadim's *And God Created Woman* starring Brigitte Bardot, Alain Resnais' *Hiroshima My Love* and the classic *Cyrano de Bergerac* starring Gérard Depardieu.

The stories of Marcel Pagnol captured on film are nostalgic visions of the countryside and of childhood in a loving family. French films have been perceived by the rest of the world as sensual, poignant, political, literary and highly personal visions of the human condition.

The French produce about 150 full-length feature films each year. The international film festival at Cannes is the most prestigious in the industry. Television and home videos are now serious rivals of the movie.

LEISURE

IN EARLIER TIMES, the typical French farmer finished a long day of vigorous activity in the fields and spent any free hours quietly. His favorite pastime was arguing politics. He relaxed by reading the paper or perhaps dozing under it.

Today, French people enjoy a shorter official work week of 39 hours, with five weeks of vacation. They often perform their labors sitting quietly at an office desk. Increasingly, they spend their leisure time plunging into active sports in the pursuit of physical fitness and "the good life."

More French schools are adding sports programs. Schools and communities are building more gyms, swimming pools and playing fields. The newly sports-minded French hope to excel in world-class sports competition, especially the Olympics.

Opposite: **Horse riding is very popular with the French. The more daring even attempt difficult stunts.**

Left: **Many people go on vacation twice a year, once in summer and once in winter. Winter vacations are usually spent skiing in the Alps.**

TEAM AND INDIVIDUAL SPORTS

The French play and watch soccer, which they call "football," in huge numbers. Each region has its own team, and there are nearly 8,000 soccer clubs. They also play basketball, volleyball and rugby football. Both men and women compete in boxing, judo and other individual contests.

The French can be quite serious about their sports, even wildly competitive. Cockfights in the north and bullfights in the south roused fierce passions in earlier times.

More popular than team sports are individual pursuits. The French ride horseback, ride bicycles, jog, ice skate, camp, hike and climb. Once up, they may choose to come back down by hang-gliding.

They head to the water to swim, sail, canoe, windsurf and water-ski. They also ski

The French love the beach, not just to swim and sunbathe, but also to practice other sports.

on snow in great numbers over vast expanses of mountainous terrain. The 1992 Winter Olympics will be hosted by Albertville in the Alps.

Tennis is no longer a sport for the rich only, as each year more public courts are being built. Golf is still fairly exclusive, played on private courses in large cities and resort areas.

Spectator sports such as horse races remain popular. Three famous auto races that create great interest are the Le Mans 24-hour race, the Monte Carlo Rally and the Grand Prix. The International Tennis Championships in Paris and the Bol d'Or motorcycle race at Le Mans also draw enthusiastic fans. The Tour de France, a 20-day bicycle race across the country, is France's most popular spectator sport.

TOUR DE FRANCE

Most daily activities all over France come to a halt during the annual Tour de France bicycle race. Millions watch it on TV or go out to join the cheering crowds lining the 2,500-mile route. Each July, close to 200 professional racers from many countries compete in this event, though around 40 drop out before the end. Each racer must belong to a team of nine riders, with varying special skills in climbing or sprinting.

This race, held for the first time in 1903, winds through many regions of France, including extremely steep mountain roads. Those who finish ride proudly down the Champs-Elysées through the Arc de Triomphe in Paris.

The cyclist with the best time at the end of each day wears the coveted yellow vest on the following day as he struggles to retain his lead. Most overall winners are French, though American Greg LeMond has won several races recently.

The Tour de France means big business. Large sums are won and lost by gamblers on the race. The winning cyclist will become a millionaire through endorsements and advertising, while makers of cars, bicycles, sports clothes and soft drinks compete to have their products appear on TV being used by the heroes of the day.

Guignol was a popular 18th-century puppet character. Today the name is used to refer to the puppet show.

OTHER LEISURE PURSUITS

French people pursue every kind of hobby, from photography to ceramics and weaving, from collecting antiques to playing musical instruments, from bird watching to stamp collecting.

Like the farmers of old, the French still hunt and fish. Both freshwater and deep sea fishing are popular.

The French also read and watch television and attend cultural events in their leisure time. They enjoy the game of Scrabble, crossword puzzles, card games, chess and bridge.

They follow Voltaire's advice to cultivate their gardens, and they spend significant amounts of time and money on improvements to their home, including their many weekend-and-vacation second homes.

In the big cities, there are lots of things to do for leisure. Especially in Paris, families visit the many large and small museums, the aquarium, the planetarium and the wax museum. Leisure in the parks is especially nice for children, who enjoy the puppet shows, donkey rides, sailing rented miniature boats on ponds, visiting zoos, and riding on carousels and miniature trains.

The French version of Punch and Judy puppet shows, known as *Théâtre Guignol* ("guee-NYOHL"), is especially popular in Lyon. Marionettes dramatize childhood fables and social and political satire in a tradition dating back to the late 1700s.

Entire families flock to Parc Astérix north of Paris every day. This theme park was inspired by the popular French cartoon strip about characters from ancient Gaul who resisted the Roman invasion of France 2,000 years ago.

The European Disneyland in Marne-la-Vallée brings an international flavor to the French leisure scene. This $4.4 billion project covers more than 5,000 acres of former sugar beet fields 20 miles east of Paris. The whole park takes up an area one-fifth the size of Paris.

Astérix is a cartoon character created by Goscinny and Uderzo a few decades ago. Modern readers of the comic strip can now mingle with the Gallic heroes at the Parc Astérix.

Both the Paris subway and the TGV bring visitors speedily to the theme park, where they can find accommodation in six hotels. Disney officials, noting that "France is the crossroads of Europe," predict 11 million visitors in the opening year, 1992. Over the next decades, Disney will add a second park based on Disney's MGM Studio Tour in Florida, office towers and convention centers, and thousands of homes, apartments and campsites.

While featuring Mickey Mouse and all the popular American attractions, Euro Disneyland has a more European flavor. The new Discoveryland is based on the science fiction of France's Jules Verne, and Snow White speaks German.

VACATIONS

Nearly half of the French population head for a beach, most often between July 14 and August 31, clogging the nation's highways. One-quarter of the French population vacation abroad, with Spain, Italy and Greece among the more popular destinations.

A great interest in health and education also spills over into the choice of leisure activities. On the highways, rest stops have been set up to include running tracks, obstacle courses and exercise equipment. Some vacation centers combine sports with such health treatments as seawater therapy and mudbaths. Center Parcs, a popular vacation village near Paris, features a swimming pool with wave machines and water slides.

The French, like foreign tourists, sometimes take hot air balloon rides through the wine country of the Loire Valley and Burgundy. They admire the countryside from barges that cruise the inland waterways.

BOULES, PÉTANQUE AND PELOTA

French men particularly enjoy *boules* ("BOOL"), a form of bowling without the pins. Each player throws two large metal balls in turn at a smaller ball. The small target ball is called *cochonnet* ("koh-shuh-NAY," the piglet), and the object is to land your ball closest to it. The rules allow for knocking the other players' balls away, and onlookers are generous with advice to the players.

Pétanque ("pay-TAHNK") is a similar bowling game played with metal balls that are thrown into the air rather than rolled along the ground. It is particularly popular in the south, where groups gather in the village square for a casual game.

In the southwest, people play the Basque game of pelota. The players may wear gloves to hit the ball against a wall.

Vacation camps are popular. The ultimate leisure camp comes from France—Club Med, which operates resorts called "villages" in many countries and attracts people from all over the world. Each Club Med offers the equipment and lessons for a great variety of sports, especially water sports. Exotic locations, sightseeing tours to such sites as Mayan ruins near Cancún in Mexico, and courses to brush up computer skills can add to the intellectual stimulation of a Club Med vacation.

FESTIVALS

WHEN FRENCH CHILDREN GROW UP to write books or make movies about their lives, some of the happiest moments they recall are of celebrating festivals with their families. Some of their celebrations are widely known outside of France: Christmas, Easter and New Year's festivities. Others, such as the Bastille Day celebration, are uniquely French. In either case, the French observe these occasions with tremendous energy and style. And, naturally, every French celebration includes the creative touch of wonderful things to eat and drink.

Opposite: **Wine festivals are called** *vendanges* **in French. The people of Bordeaux, a town well-known for its wine, break out in joyous celebration during the** *vendanges.*

ELEVEN HOLIDAYS

There are 11 legal holidays in France representing religious, national and historic reasons for celebration. The six religious holidays reflect France's Roman Catholic history. These include *Pâques* (Easter, a Monday in March or April), Ascension Day (a Thursday in May), Pentecost (the seventh Monday after Easter, in May or June), the Feast of the Assumption (August 15), *Toussaint* ("too-SAN," All Saints' Day, November 1) and *Noël* (Christmas, December 25).

HOLIDAYS FOR THE FAMILY

A holiday especially for children is celebrated on January 6, Epiphany, which coincides with Twelfth Night, 12 nights after Christmas. A large round pastry called *la galette des rois* ("lah gah-LEHT day RWAH," the cake of kings) containing a single bean is served. The youngest child present cuts the cake and passes out the pieces. Whoever finds the bean becomes the king or queen for the holiday and chooses a royal mate.

February 2 is celebrated as Candlemas, a religious holiday involving a mass with candles carried in a procession. Families cook thin pancakes called *crêpes*, and everyone tries flipping them. Legend has it that flipping the *crêpes* while holding a coin will bring happiness and wealth.

Parades and fireworks are the order of the day on Bastille Day.

Civil holidays include New Year's Day on January 1 and Labor Day on May 1, and three additional dates that mark historical events.

Bastille Day, July 14, commemorates the storming of the Bastille prison in 1789, an event that sparked off the French Revolution. Also known as Le Quatorze Juillet ("luh kah-TORZ zhwee-YAY," July 14), this day is also France's national holiday. Tricolor flags appear on monuments and buses. In Paris, military troops parade past the country's president. After dark, the skies blaze with fireworks, and crowds of people dance in the streets.

A particularly spirited observance of this holiday in the medieval walled town of Carcassonne in the south of the country is enriched by spectacular fireworks and a festival of music, theater and dance that lasts for two weeks.

Armistice Day, November 11, commemorates the end of World War I in 1918. Victory Day, May 8, celebrates the end of World War II in 1945. This holiday is sometimes called the Day of Liberty and Peace.

HOLIDAY REVELRY

Celebrations around Christmas and New Year's Day are particularly joyous. On Christmas Eve, families gather to feast on turkey and, for dessert, a traditional Yule log, the *bûche de Noël* ("BOOSH duh noh-EL"). Old and young share gifts, as in Christian countries around the world.

Sometimes children put out their shoes at bedtime, and Father Christmas fills them with gifts during the night. Naughty children get only a whip instead of toys, delivered by le Père Fouettard ("luh PEHR foo-eh-TAHR"), the Whip Father.

It was in the French province of Alsace that Christmas trees first appeared in 1605. By the 19th century, they had become popular all over Europe and in the United States. In the mountains at Christmas, skiers light up the night by descending with flaming torches.

New Year's Eve is celebrated with a feast and the honking of car horns at midnight. The following day, people wish each other a Happy New Year and exchange gifts meant to bring good luck.

Carnival (Mardi Gras) is celebrated in many French cities on Shrove Tuesday, the last day before the Catholic observance of Lent. The observance of Carnival in Nice, on the French Riviera, began sometime in the 13th century. Today, partying goes on for weeks with evening torchlight processions and parades of flower-covered floats and huge groups of papier-mâché "big heads." Masked balls, confetti battles, flower-tossing and fireworks lead up to the moment when a model of "King Carnival" is set on fire, hanged or drowned.

Mardi Gras has a carnival spirit as young people dress up in fancy dress and party all night long.

Right: **For Christians, Easter is a time of rejoicing. Everybody goes to church and children are given chocolate eggs.**

Below: **A paper fish is stuck on the back of unsuspecting persons on April Fool's Day.**

April 1 is celebrated as *Poisson d'Avril* ("pwah-SAWN dahv-REEL," April Fish). This is something like April Fool's Day in the United States. In France, people try to pin a paper fish on someone's back without being caught. Then, they laugh and point to the "victim," calling, *"Poisson d'avril!"* The person who is fooled is supposed to give the pranksters a chocolate fish.

Legend traces this holiday back to 1564, when Charles IX switched the beginning of the year from April 1 back to January 1. People protested mildly by exchanging silly gifts and playing pranks. Since the sun at the time was in Pisces (the zodiac sign featuring two fish), candy fish as well as paper fish became associated with the holiday.

On Easter Monday, French children receive colored candy eggs and chocolate chickens. They may go to church in their best outfits and later hunt for Easter eggs. No church bells are rung between Good Friday and Easter Sunday.

On Labor Day, people exchange lilies of the valley and wear a blossom for good luck.

REGIONAL FESTIVALS AND SEASONAL EVENTS

Many areas of France have colorful festivals throughout the year.

In Brittany, Quimper's Festival de Cornouaille, held every year since 1923, recalls the pre-Christian civilization of that region. Puppets act out Celtic tales, women demonstrate their embroidery skills, young girls model traditional lace headdresses, men engage in Breton wrestling matches, and people feast on grilled sardines and Breton *crêpes* while listening to bagpipe music and watching clog-stomping dancers.

A traditional festival in Burgundy features a jousting contest on the Yonne River. Two men carrying poles and shields stand in long boats. As the boats are rowed toward one another at full speed, each contestant tries to push the other one into the water.

In Brittany, men, women and children wear their charming traditional dress during local festivals.

In Verdigny, the Fête des Grappes Nouvelles celebrates the end of the harvest. Wine-tasters in ceremonial dress sample the wines solemnly.

In Alsace, a medieval festival at Ribeauvillé features knights in armor jousting, simulated bearbaiting, and parades of people grandly dressed as noble lords and ladies.

The Riviera city of Cannes welcomes some 40,000 film professionals to perhaps the most important film festival of the calendar year. The judges at Cannes review films from many countries, and their awards are reported in newspapers all over the world. Glamorous people-watching is an added attraction at this two-week festival.

Les Trois Glorieuses ("LAY TRWAH glaw-ree-YUHZ," the three glorious days) in November is France's chief wine festival, one of many autumn harvest festivals. Three cities in Burgundy share the honors, and all are world-famous in wine-tasting circles: Beaune, Clos-de-Vougeot and Meursault. After the year's most important wine auction, professionals and amateurs alike indulge in spirited wine-tasting and folk-dancing.

Wine-growers and drinkers also celebrate the appearance of the Beaujolais Nouveau (new red wine) in November. Grape harvest festivals, known as *vendanges* ("vawhn-DAHNZH"), are widely celebrated. Members of old wine societies wear traditional costumes, and everyone tastes wine and dances. Even when it's not harvest time, the French can find a reason to rejoice. The wine villages pay tribute to their patron saint on St. Vincent's Day, January 22.

In addition to the grapevine, harvest festivals honor other gifts of the land: peaches in Roussillon, lavender in Digne and apple cider in Normandy.

The long summer vacations enjoyed by French children and their families also coincide with festivals in many southern cities. Elaborate programs of concerts and plays, folk dancing, parades and feasting attract French and foreign tourists.

France has nearly 500 summer music festivals, ranging from concerts on boats and in churches and historic *châteaux* to organ festivals in cathedrals with famous old organs, to festivals devoted to folk music or chamber music or jazz.

Paris celebrates summer with the Festival of the Marais (a city neighborhood) from mid-June to mid-July with music, dance and drama. Later in the summer, during the Festival Estival, Parisians enjoy classical concerts in churches, museums and concert halls around the city. The Festival of Autumn continues Paris' arts celebrations through the fall months, with special emphasis on contemporary music.

Outside France proper but within easy celebrating distance are major festivals of Monaco: the International Circus Festival and the Monte Carlo Motor Rally in January, the Monaco Grand Prix (horse racing) in May, and the International Fireworks Festival in mid-summer.

Many festivals in France celebrate major events in the Catholic Church. Most villages honor their patron saint with a festival in July.

LES SAINTES

An unusual gathering takes place near the end of May in the Mediterranean village of Saintes-Maries-de-la-Mer in the Camargue. Many thousands of Gypsies come from all over Europe to honor their patron saint, Sarah of Egypt. They hold a candlelight vigil and a march to the sea carrying holy statues of their saints in a carved boat. In a region already known for colorful bullfights, flamingos and wild horses, the Gypsies add the dramatic finishing touch.

Another pilgrimage in October also attracts many pilgrims and thousands of onlookers.

FOOD

THE FRENCH PEOPLE care passionately about food. From rich to poor, from aristocrat to laborer, they invest significant time and money in the pursuit of fine meals.

Great care is given to the raw materials of a good meal. Each person involved in the growing, marketing and preparation of food is an important and respected link in the chain that produces food in France. Generations of families devote themselves to producing exquisite cheeses, fruits and vegetables. They breed special strains of chickens, ducks and geese, and cows, sheep and hogs to better satisfy the demanding French housewives and restaurant patrons.

The French have written extensively about food for centuries, so that the cuisine is a rich field for study, with its own encyclopedias and histories full of original culinary geniuses, showmen and dynamic personalities. Rating restaurants is a national sport, and numerous guides on the subject are published each year.

The result is a cuisine that has greatly influenced the food of other lands. International wine and food societies celebrate the recipes of France's greatest chefs. The export of French foodstuffs and wines is big business, bringing important foreign exchange and prestige to France.

Opposite: **France is well-known for its dairy products which are exported to many parts of the world.**

Above: **French cooks insist on the freshest vegetables for their dishes.**

TYPES OF CUISINE

There are many types of meals to enjoy in France, depending on what you can spend, where you are, and what you feel like eating. The most elaborate style of cooking, *haute cuisine*, describes the grand meal of many courses served by top restaurants.

The hearty meals a housewife cooks for her family are known as *cuisine bourgeoise* which overlaps with *cuisine régionale* ("ray-zhuh-NAHL"), or regional cooking—dishes made from locally available ingredients served in the provinces.

In certain restaurants, the chef offers a set menu with many courses of fairly small portions, giving a sampler of the chef's specialties and the best foods of the season and the region.

Nouvelle cuisine refers to a recent trend among French chefs to serve lighter food with little or no butter, cream or flour in the sauces. Food is arranged artistically on the plate, which may be decorated with edible flowers. Meats and vegetables are undercooked rather than overcooked. The low-calorie dishes of *cuisine minceur* ("man-SOOR") were created in an attempt to fuse dieting and weight-control with fine French cooking.

REGIONAL FOODS AND DISHES

Different regions of France are famous for unique and special foods that come from that area only, and for regional styles of cooking. Regional recipes are often passed down from one generation to the next, preserved on family stoves and in the kitchens of inns and restaurants throughout the provinces.

Oysters from Brittany are prized for their delicate flavor.

The highly-prized ingredients and distinctive styles of regional cuisines can also be sampled in Paris which, like any other cosmopolitan city, offers a wide variety of foods. However the prices of regional dishes are much higher in Paris than in the provinces. The French people enjoy seeking good regional cooking in the provinces where the ducks are actually fattened, the fish caught or the truffles unearthed.

There are foods of almost unlimited variety and thousands of ways to prepare them throughout France. Some French foods that may be unfamiliar to foreigners include sea urchins, eel, snails, brains, kidneys, the entire calf's head, pig's trotters, little birds like woodcock and thrush, and all kinds of wild game.

In general, the cooking of northern France is based on butter, while southern French cooking uses olive oil, as does neighboring Italy.

One of the most famous regional foods of France, *pâté de foie gras* ("pah-TAY duh FWAH GRAH"), the famous liver spread made from specially fattened ducks or geese, comes from Périgord in southwestern France and also from Alsace.

The waters of the Channel and the Atlantic Coast yield many varieties of mussels, oysters and fish. From Provence come olives and herbs—bay leaf, fennel, rosemary and thyme. Excellent pork dishes—hams, pâtés, terrines and sausages known collectively as *charcuterie*—differ from one region of France to another.

A famous white or pink chewy candy filled with chopped almonds and cherries, called *nougat*, comes from the town of Montélimar. Dijon exports several styles of mustard. Privas near Lyon produces *marron glacés* ("mah-ROHN glah-SAY"), a delicacy of candied chestnuts. The region of Burgundy is known for snails, Cavaillon for melons, Normandy for butter, cream, cheese and sparkling cider.

"BLACK DIAMONDS": TRUFFLES (mushrooms)

The cult of the truffle is unique to France. This black, warty fungus grows underground in the roots of oak and hazelnut trees. Trained dogs and pigs are adept at sniffing out these hidden treasures. Because they have not yet been successfully cultivated by farmers, truffles are rare. Scientists are trying to develop a machine to hunt them, claiming that pigs and dogs miss 80% of those in the ground.

Truffles are served whole or minced in sauces, eggs and other dishes, and provide a nutty flavor adored by the French. They are tastier fresh than canned, but are very costly either way, as much as $650 a pound for the best truffles from Périgord.

French food-lovers and foreign tourists travel to Mont-Saint-Michel in Normandy to sample the famous local omelets. They seek the finest *bouillabaisse* ("boo-ya-BESS"), a fragrant fish stew, in Marseilles. They head west to Toulouse to sample the perfect *cassoulet* ("kah-soo-LAY"), a complex casserole of white beans, lamb, pork, sausage and poultry.

The origin of many a recipe is revealed in its name: frog legs provençal, from the province of Provence; salad niçoise, with olives, anchovies, tomatoes and tuna, from the city of Nice; beef bourguignon, beef stew with onions and mushrooms simmered in red wine, from the province of Burgundy; quiche lorraine, a custard tart with bacon and cheese, from the province of Lorraine; calf's head à la lyonnaise, with chopped onions and parsley as served in the city of Lyon; and veal à la normande, made with cream and Calvados apple brandy of Normandy.

Provençal dishes often contain onions, garlic, tomatoes and olives. An Alsatian dish, on the other hand, probably has sauerkraut somewhere in the recipe, and is washed down with beer instead of wine. Périgourdine ("pay-ree-gohr-DEEN") means there are luscious and expensive black truffles from Périgord in the sauce.

The cheeses of France often bear the name of the town where they are made, such as the world-famous blue-veined Roquefort made from ewe's milk and ripened in caves. France is known for Camembert, Brie, Port Salut ("POR sah-LEWH"), and more than 300 other kinds of cheeses, many of which are exported around the world. The various cheeses made from goats' milk are called *chèvres* ("SHEVR").

French cheese comes in a variety of shapes and flavors.

CAFÉS, BRASSERIES, BISTROS

The habit of sitting at a café table for gossip and socializing is deeply ingrained in French society.

There are many wonderful places to eat in France. Cafés offer drinks and snacks and, in the larger cities, light meals. They may have outdoor seats along the sidewalk. They are open long hours, sometimes around the clock, making them the popular spot to linger for gossip and perhaps a game of chess, dominoes or table football.

Bistros range from simple bars to time-honored old restaurants with faithful patrons. Reflected in the decorated mirrors, waiters in blue aprons serve house specialties, omelets, steak with fries and sometimes much fancier foods.

The neighborhood café or *bistro* may be an endangered species, however, since so many are converting into fast-food places or fashionable restaurants. France had 107,000 *bistros* in 1980, and only about 80,000 in 1990.

Brasseries are large, busy restaurants with waiters in white aprons. Traditionally, a *brasserie* brewed beer; the cuisine is on the heavier side, with many Alsatian and seafood dishes.

An *auberge* ("oh-BEHRZH") is an inn, usually in the country, serving drinks and complete meals.

Customary hours for most French restaurants are noon to 2:30 p.m. and 7:00 to 9:30 p.m., with later closings in Paris. Menus with prices are often freshly hand-written each day and are posted outside the restaurants.

These mouth-watering pastries can be bought from any *pâtisserie* in town. They are generally of very good quality.

EATING THROUGH THE DAY

In France, families start the day with a small breakfast. Everyone has bread, butter and jam. They drink black coffee, coffee with hot milk or the children's favorite—hot chocolate. Flaky, crescent-shaped rolls called *croissants* appear as a treat on Sundays.

The main meal of the day is often eaten at noon during the two-hour lunch break. It consists of several courses, beginning with an appetizer or soup. Steaks with French-fried potatoes or roast chicken served with vegetables are popular main courses.

The salad, usually made of greens tossed with oil-and-vinegar dressing, follows as a separate course. A selection of cheeses may come next, and then fresh fruit or a pastry dessert to complete the meal.

Sunday dinners and grand occasions call for impressive desserts, such as the famed French pastries in a dazzling variety of shapes and flavors. Popular choices are fruit tarts, éclairs and thin pancakes with sweet fillings. There are regional specialties and also desserts reserved for certain holidays and celebrations.

Long, crisp loaves of French bread, called *baguettes*, accompany meals. Because this bread has no preservatives, the French buy it fresh each day. *Brioches* are a popular sweet, soft round dinner bun. Wine is usually served at lunch and dinner. Mineral water, either plain or carbonated, may also be drunk. At festive meals, a different wine may be served with each course, and after-dinner brandies or sweet drinks called liqueurs may be offered, along with strong black coffee served in small cups. The French add sugar but not cream to this coffee. At a very formal meal, a fish course comes between the appetizer and the meat course.

People who do not go home for the midday meal may eat a lighter lunch of a quiche or sandwich in a restaurant.

The evening meal, whether called dinner or supper, may be simpler than the large midday meal. A typical menu would be soup, a casserole, and bread and cheese.

At meals, the French, like most Europeans, cut food with the fork in their left hand and the knife in their right. They do not then switch the fork to the right hand to eat, as people do in the United States, nor will they use a knife to cut large salad greens. They break off chunks of bread instead of slicing the *baguette*.

France produces a quarter of the world's wines and the French are the biggest drinkers of wine per capita in the world.

WINES AND OTHER SPIRITS

France is famous for its excellent wines and bubbly champagnes. There are several important wine-producing regions, and each one makes a unique kind of wine. The shape of its bottle tells where a wine was made: Burgundy, Bordeaux, Alsace, Provence or the Rhône Valley.

The year on a bottle is important because changing weather conditions always affect the flavor of the grapes. The prices also vary from year to year, with the greatest wines costing hundreds of dollars per bottle. Ordinary table wines are quite inexpensive.

Some wines improve with age and must rest in their bottles for years. Others can be drunk young. Many vineyards maintain huge wine cellars and offer tastings to the public in their tasting cellars.

Because French wines are so important to French prestige and the economy, the government inspects them to maintain their quality. Labels with the letters "A.O.C." indicate that a wine has been officially approved.

Beer and cider are also produced in France. Other drinks, called *apéritifs* ("ah-pay-ree-TEEF") are drunk before meals. *Pernod* and *pastis* have an anise flavor and are quite popular. After-dinner brandies such as armagnac and cognac are also commonly drunk.

FRANCE

A   B   C   D

1

BELGIUM

Lille

NORD-PAS-DE-CALAIS

GERMANY

English Channel

LUXEMBOURG

UPPER NORMANDY

PICARDY

2

LOWER NORMANDY

Seine River

Rouen

Paris

LORRAINE

Strasbourg

BRITTANY

ILE-DE-FRANCE

CHAMPAGNE-ARDENNE

ALSACE

Seine River

Marne River

Orléans

Loire River

PAYS DE LA LOIRE

Blois

FRANCHE-COMTÉ

Loire River

Tours

CENTER

BURGUNDY

SWITZER-LAND

3

La Rochelle

POITOU-CHARENTES

LIMOUSIN

Saône River

Annecy

▲ Mont Blanc

Limoges

AUVERGNE

Lyon

Grenoble

Bay of Biscay

RHÔNE-ALPES

ITALY

Bordeaux

Dordogne River

Garonne River

Rhône River

PROVENCE-ALPES-CÔTE D'AZUR

4

AQUITAINE

MIDI-PYRÉNÉES

Toulon

Nîmes

Carcassonne

Marseilles

LANGUEDOC-ROUSSILLON

Nice Monaco

Perpignan

Mediterranean Sea

CORSICA

SPAIN

5

Ajaccio

N
↑

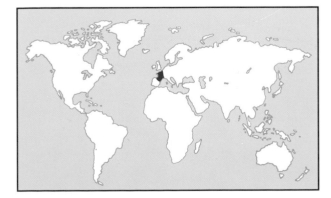

International Boundary
State Boundary
▲ Mountain
● Capital
• City
⋏ River

QUICK NOTES

LAND AREA
210,026 square miles (including Corsica)

POPULATION
56 million

CAPITAL
Paris

REGIONS
Alsace, Aquitaine, Auvergne, Burgundy, Brittany, Center, Champagne-Ardenne, Corsica, Franche-Comté, Ile-de-France, Languedoc-Roussillon, Limousin, Lorraine, Lower Normandy, Midi-Pyrénées, Nord-Pas-de-Calais, Pays de la Loire, Picardy, Poitou-Charentes, Provence-Alpes-Côte d'Azur, Rhône-Alpes, Upper Normandy, overseas departments and territories.

LONGEST RIVER
Loire River (632.5 miles)

HIGHEST POINT
Mont Blanc (15,771 feet)

NATIONAL ANTHEM
La Marseillaise

NATIONAL LANGUAGE
French

NATIONAL MOTTO
Liberty, equality, fraternity

MAJOR RELIGION
Roman Catholic

CURRENCY
French franc, divided into 100 centimes (US$1 = 5.8FF)

MEASUREMENTS
Metric system

MAIN EXPORTS
Chemicals, machinery, electrical and electronic equipment, automobiles, aircraft, weapons, wine, foodstuffs, agricultural products, iron and steel

IMPORTANT ANNIVERSARIES
Bastille Day (July 14), Labor Day (May 1), Victory Day (May 8), Armistice Day (November 11)

LEADERS IN POLITICS
Napoleon Bonaparte (1769–1821), First Consul (1799–1804) and Emperor of France (1804–1814 and again in 1815); brilliant military leader; founded French legal system (Code Napoleon); reorganized education

Charles de Gaulle (1890–1970) led French resistance from exile against Germany in World War II; rebuilt French glory and restored order as president of Fifth Republic from 1958 until his resignation in 1969

Georges Pompidou (1911–1974), premier of France (1962–1968); president of Fifth French Republic (1969–1974); continued policies initiated by De Gaulle

François Mitterrand (b. 1916), Socialist president of Fifth French Republic (1981–)

GLOSSARY

baguette   Long loaf of French bread.

boules   Game of bowling without pins popular in southern France.

bourgeoisie   Dominant class in France today, made up of professionals and business leaders.

château   Castle, grand country home once belonging to a king, queen or noble family.

crêpes   Thin pancakes.

football   Soccer.

gendarmes   State police serving in the armed forces.

guignol   Puppet show dramatizing childhood fables.

guillotine   Instrument of execution by beheading.

joie de vivre   Love of life, joy in living.

savoir-faire   Ability to do or say the right thing in any given situation.

BIBLIOGRAPHY

Macaulay, David: *Cathedral; The Story of Its Construction*, Houghton Mifflin Co., Boston, 1973.
Mayle, Peter: *A Year in Provence*, Hamish Hamilton Ltd., London, 1989, and Alfred A. Knopf, Inc., New York, 1990.
Mitchell, Crohan: *The Napoleonic Wars*, David and Charles, New York, 1989.
Mulvahill, Margaret: *The French Revolution*, Franklin Watts, New York, 1989.
Tomlins, James: *We Live in France*, the Bookwright Press, New York, 1983.
Ventura, Piero: *Great Painters*, G.P. Putnam's Sons, New York, 1984.

INDEX